THE LANGUAGE EFFECT

Why **AI-Powered Copywriting** is a marketer's (new) best friend

Parry Malm

Published by Known Publishing, 2020.

978-1-913036-10-2

All facts correct at time of publication.

KNOWN

www.get-known.co.uk

Illustrations designed by Amy Davis & Spencer Peppiatt

Editing by Stu Elmes, Verity Jennings & Leila Green

To my wee son Axel, who, every time I think I'm a big deal, brings me back down to earth by looking me right in the eye while he shits himself.

ABOUT THE AUTHOR

PARRY MALM
CO-FOUNDER AND CEO, PHRASEE

Parry Malm is co-founder and CEO of Phrasee, and is the pioneer of AI-Powered Copywriting. He took what many called an impossible idea – a machine that writes better than humans – and turned it into reality. Before that, he was an accomplished brand-side marketer and learned firsthand the impact of powerful copy – and how, when left to his own (human) devices, he'd never be the best.

Raised in Vancouver, Canada, he earned a Bachelor of Business Administration before moving to London, England, in 2006. He currently lives in Tooting, south London, with his wife and their son. In his spare time, he enjoys watching grown men on skates punch each other in the face (or as they call it outside of Canada, ice hockey). And he likes Megadeth. A lot.

Find out more about the author and the team behind Phrasee at: **phrasee.co**

BEFORE I DIVE IN, THIS BOOK IS FOR YOU IF:

- You want to deliver better marketing results
- You realize that digital channels are the future of marketing
- You'd like better digital marketing performance for your brand
- You think your digital marketing copy could be better
- Your brand could use more engagement
- You want to build a more effective digital marketing strategy
- You want to increase your conversion rates
- You want to lead the pack, be an early adopter, and be years ahead of the mainstream
- You want the kudos (and promotion) associated with being the game changer in your company's marketing department
- You're ready to reinvent how your brand uses copy to deliver better performance.

My name is Parry Malm, and I'm here to show you the future...

That is, I'm here to help you answer these questions: is the marketing copy you use effective enough? What can you do to make your digital marketing processes more efficient and productive? How can you get better results without resorting to clickbait or spam? What can technology do to enable this process?

If you seek the answers to those questions, then you've come to the right place.

Buckle up, because the future is going to be wild.

WHAT TO EXPECT IN THIS BOOK

The Language Effect and its enabler, AI-Powered Copywriting, are novel concepts. They're concepts derived from a combination of economics, linguistics, and technology. They're concepts that challenge your existing ways of thinking. They're concepts that will make you money.

But as these are so new – and challenge the status quo – explaining them requires deep-dives into a number of areas. So, I've divided this book into four sections to equip you with the knowledge and tools you need to revolutionize how you market your brand.

Part 1, Why Killer Copy is Your Superpower, explains the transformative power of better language in your marketing campaigns… and, conversely, the cost of ineffective language. It also outlines the economic disequilibrium we have found ourselves in and how, thus far, it's led us down the clickbait race to the bottom. But it doesn't have to be this way.

Part 2, Why You Need to Throw Out the Old Rule Book, looks at the bygone era of Don Drapers, and why you can no longer let them dictate your discourse. It looks at the fallibility of human intuition, and the infinite complexity of human language. Then, I outline a simple, proven formula to measure the revenue impact of The Language Effect.

Part 3, Getting Started with AI-Powered Copywriting, is all about the tech. We'll run through the options available in the market today and the benefits of each. I'll also explain why your brand's voice is so important, and how you can prevent it from being diluted.

Part 4, The History and Future of The Language Effect, prevails upon the notion that we must remember the past to avoid repeating its mistakes. We look at several analogous examples of disruptive technology, and then culminate with my Marketing Manifesto – a call to arms that asks you the provocative question: are you a marketer of the past, or a marketer of the future?

Each part can stand on its own, and each part will make sense in isolation. However, I'd urge you to consume the book front-to-back. I've spent countless hours crafting the narrative journey, and I think you'll enjoy it.

So, with no further ado, I present to you the future of marketing. The future of copywriting. The future of your career.

I present to you **The Language Effect: Why AI-Powered Copywriting is a marketer's (new) best friend.**

BEFORE WE START, LET ME DROP SOME SCIENCE...

WHAT IS THE LANGUAGE EFFECT?

The Language Effect (n): the measurable impact that better copy has on your brand's marketing campaigns.

From an early age, I realized the effect of language. I was five years old, and my older cousin Shawn taught me my first ever swearword. After I unwittingly said it to my mom, and subsequently dealt with the consequences, I learned that there was great power within language... and this lesson I've carried with me for my entire life.

Throughout my career, first as a brand-side marketer, and now as CEO of one of the world's fastest-growing AI companies, I've always been very particular about the language I use, because I know the right phrasing will make me money... and the wrong phrasing will do the opposite.

And it's the same for you! The impact of powerful copy in your marketing campaigns is unparalleled. But, frustratingly, until now, your only option was to choose that copy based on gut instinct, or worse, the whims of self-proclaimed 'experts'.

But what if you applied the same level of scientific rigor to your copy that you do in every other aspect of your marketing mix?

That's what this book is all about – how optimizing the copy you use… and meticulously measuring it… will make you millions.

It's the phenomenon that will galvanize your brand… your team… your targets… and your career.

It's The Language Effect. And it's yours to seize.

> **'Phrasee makes you money, so you're likely to get your bonus.'**
>
> *Gareth Jones, CMO, eBay*

WHAT IS AI-POWERED COPYWRITING?

AI-Powered Copywriting (n): using artificial intelligence to create better copy for your brand than humans can write alone.

The Language Effect is real, it is proven, and it can be yours.

But to reap the benefits of the effect, you need a cause… and the cause of this lucrative effect is AI-Powered Copywriting.

What is AI-Powered Copywriting? It's a set of AI tools that generate high-performing marketing copy… proven higher-performing copy than humans can write when left to their own devices.

And that's awesome in itself. But what AI-Powered Copywriting actually does is much more profound.

Imagine you had the ability to turn everyone on your team into one of the world's best copywriters. And they never had bad days, never took vacations, and always did exactly what you asked.

That's what AI-Powered Copywriting does: it gives you access to the smartest, most impactful copywriting in the world, all at the click of a button.

It is the one technology you need to experience The Language Effect.

AI-Powered Copywriting is the future of marketing… and the future is NOW.

> **'Week one, we saw positive results. Week two, we saw positive results. In week three, I said, "Now we have a trend." Day after day Phrasee proved out.'**
>
> *Lee Washington II,*
> *CRM & Loyalty Strategy Manager, JOANN Stores*

TABLE OF CONTENTS

PART 3
GETTING STARTED WITH AI-POWERED COPYWRITING

PART 4
THE FUTURE OF MARKETING

INTRODUCTION: HOW AI-POWERED COPYWRITING WAS BORN

F*CK YOU, PARRY

When that text message buzzed on my phone on a cool fall morning in 2013, I had no idea how much it would change my life.

I read it again. 'F*ck you, Parry.' Yup, I read that right the first time. The number I didn't recognize – it was from a UK cell phone, but aside from that, I had no idea who it was.

I quickly reviewed the last 24 hours of my life. Had I inadvertently upset someone? Perhaps their grievance was from before yesterday. I racked my brain. I had no idea who the message was from, or what it was about.

I was taken aback, though.

I took a sip of the tepid water in the pint glass on my bedside and dragged myself into the shower. I ruminated over the text. Who could be so annoyed at me that they'd send me such a visceral message at six in the morning?

I toweled myself off, got dressed, and grabbed my backpack. The door closed behind me and I walked over to Tooting Broadway station in south London. I hopped onto the Northern line. It was busy that morning – busier than usual. Throughout the inhospitable morning commute, my mind went over and over the possibilities, but I still couldn't figure out that text.

I got to the office, preoccupied by the strange text message. I mean, I'm no angel, and I've ticked off my fair share of men and women over the years – who hasn't?

But what had I done to deserve this?

I sat down and gazed across my desk to my co-worker Andrew, who headed up the sales team. He looked at me with a smirk, and in a strong North-East English accent said, 'You're a real $&#%, you know that?' I immediately realized it was he who had texted me that morning.

Taken aback, I feigned ignorance while analyzing the facts. Andrew and I worked quite closely together and were certainly collegial. But had I done something to annoy him?

He was a pretty easy-going guy normally, so I must have done something pretty bad.

But what could it have been?

My mind blanked.

And then he told me.

It was at that exact moment I had the idea to start Phrasee.

CHEATING ON MY HOMEWORK

In truth, the story of Phrasee started long before that morning. Probably from the time of my birth. My mother was a language teacher who rose to become president of her local teacher's union. My father was a physicist-turned-inventor who took an AI product to market way back in the 1990s. So perhaps I was predestined to combine these two seemingly disparate pursuits – language and technology.

Who knows?

The first time I thought about combining science and language was during my first semester at university in scenic Victoria, British Columbia, Canada. This was back in the winter of 1997; I enrolled late after a 6-month sojourn to find myself.

All I found out about myself during that sojourn, mind you, was that I wanted to go to university.

As a result of my delayed enrollment, all the easy courses for a freshman were full. So, I wound up taking calculus, computer science, and linguistics. Who could have predicted that, more than 20 years later, I'd found a company that combined the three distinct topics of my first ever university semester?

The linguistics course I took was very niche; it specifically focused on the etymology of the English language, with a particular focus on Greek and Latin. One assignment was to take a piece of prose, and identify which words were derived from Greek, Latin, or some other language. Of course, this seemed like a lot of work to me, so I developed a simple computer program that would take text as an input and the output would be a probability estimate of each word being derived from Greek, Latin, or some other language. It wasn't perfect, but it was good enough to circumvent a whole lot of repetitive work… and I wound up getting an A.

I suppose this means that the idea of applying advanced computing to language is something that has piqued my intellectual curiosity for over 20 years.

MOVING INTO MARKETING

Fast-forward to 2008, and life found me in Amsterdam, running the marketing for a division of a huge multinational media conglomerate. I managed a 7-figure marketing budget. Between the C-suite breathing down my neck pressing me for results, the IT team slowing down my ambitious plans, and the commercial team complaining about everything else, I quickly learned how to get stuff done: make the biggest impact you can, with the least involvement of other departments as possible.

One solution, which didn't need C-suite signoff, required no big IT requirements, and would deliver provable results, was obvious. We would send out millions of emails to millions of people. So, of course, I insisted first that we tested the subject lines for every single campaign before we sent it.

I analyzed these test results and performance data and attempted to build a very basic predictive model in Excel. I wanted to be able to predict how well a subject line would perform in the wild, at scale, and repeatably. I tried, oh how I tried… yet, sadly, to no avail. I couldn't predict what would work from one week to the next with any greater accuracy than blindly throwing darts at the wall and praying for a bullseye.

Fast-forward a few more years. I found myself working for an email marketing service provider in London. I was running the company's account management department and flew around the world meeting hundreds – probably thousands – of email marketers. The #1 question the folks I met would ask me was: 'what's a good subject line?'

I never had a good answer. I'd just say, 'Try out a bunch of stuff and see what works.' It felt like a cop-out. It felt intellectually impure. I knew there had to be a better way.

So, one day, I was in that ESP company's headquarters in Oxford, England, and I got chatting with the head developer. We hit it off and he offered to buy me a beer after work.

Settled in a cute Oxford pub, I asked him if he could download me a bunch of subject lines, and their associated open, click, conversion, and unsubscribe rates. He asked me why, and I didn't have a good answer. I wasn't quite sure what I'd do with the information, but I figured I could do something. Luckily, he liked me, and so the next morning I had access to a ton of data.

I started playing with the reams of data I was given and thinking of different ways to crunch it. I spent hours and hours looking at a huge number of different variables – but none of them led to much. I finally settled upon a very simple thing – a subject line keyword checker. This would take a word and compare the response rates of subject lines with that word to those without it.

To be honest, the statistics it generated weren't particularly useful, and I won't bore you with the details[1]. In hindsight, I could have done it better. Maybe I should have studied statistics in that first semester in 1997[2]. It was interesting, however, to see how seemingly small changes to a subject line's language could have a big effect on its performance when tested at scale. So, I listed out about 180 commonly used keywords to check, pulled down the tables of data, and morphed it into a 20-page report.

I stuck the report up on our company website, wrote a blog post about it, and went to sleep.

The next morning, I got that 'F*ck you' text from Andrew.

Why?

Between the time I'd published my blog post about email subject lines and the time I'd woken up the following morning, it had gone viral. The report was referenced by several media outlets – both trade press and mainstream. It even got featured in the *Financial Times*[3].

'Are you serious?! All this for email subject lines?' I thought to myself.

Now, about that text message...

The reason why Andrew was mad at me was this: the report I'd published required curious readers to enter their email address to download it. Each time one was downloaded, it would trigger him an email notification. Within the first 12 hours, it was downloaded over 10,000 times. His inbox broke – the irony of an email company's inbox breaking wasn't lost on us. He was mad because there was TOO

MUCH interest in what I had produced – more interest than he was set up to handle.

That's what they call a 'light bulb moment'. Or, perhaps, a moment of clarity. I realized that marketers had traditionally relied upon their intuition and gut instinct when it came to choosing the best language to use. The data I'd found had shown that approach to be both inefficient and ineffective, as people chose words with no appreciation of their historic performance.

The market was ready for a better approach to copywriting. It was ready to adopt advanced technology to optimize the language in marketing campaigns.

The market was ready for Phrasee.

PHRASEE WAS BORN

Since that fateful day, I, along with my two co-founders, Dr. Neil Yager – who I sat next to in my first ever computer science class way back in university, and is probably the single smartest AI mind I've ever met – and Victoria Peppiatt – who is such a branding genius that in 2008, when I ran a big corporate's marketing team, I fired a huge agency to bring her expertise in – have made it my mission to build the world's most advanced AI-Powered Copywriting technology from the ground up.

Together, we took a tiny problem – email subject lines – and turned it into big business. Phrasee now optimizes marketing language across numerous channels – from Facebook ads to push notifications and more – in 24 languages.

To date, Phrasee has:

- optimized millions of words of marketing copy
- reached over 300 million people around the world – most of them without even realizing it
- delivered increased engagement, conversions, and ROI for many of the world's biggest brands.

NEVER LET OLD WAYS OF THINKING DICTATE HOW YOU THINK TODAY

But this book isn't just about the Phrasee success story. This book is about my lifelong belief that the language we use in marketing needs to be better – and why using AI technology to make it better is the only scalable and sustainable way to make it happen.

My father – the physicist and inventor – always used to tell me, 'Never let old ways of thinking dictate how you think yourself.'

He was, and still is, right.

See, for far too long, marketers have relied upon their gut instinct to make decisions about language. 'Only humans can write copy for marketing campaigns,' the thinking went.

No one believed a machine could do it better.

They sure as hell do now.

In this book, I'm going to share with you everything you need to know to empower your brand's marketing through AI-Powered Copywriting and start seeing results... including:

- why copy is way more important than it gets credit for
- why it's so hard for even good copywriters to perfect
- how it's so much easier when you use AI technology
- what marketers need to do now to lead the parade.

You'll learn about The Language Effect – and how the marketer of the future can use it to their advantage.

The accompanying website for the book can be found at: **thelanguageeffect.com**.

"THE MARKET WAS READY FOR A BETTER APPROACH TO COPYWRITING... THE MARKET WAS READY FOR PHRASEE."

PART 1

WHY KILLER COPY IS YOUR SUPERPOWER

'In every dingy basement
on every dingy street

Every draggin' handclap
over every draggin' beat

That's just the beat of time,
beat that must go on

If you've been tryin' for years
we already heard your song'

Death or Glory
The Clash

1

GREAT MARKETING LANGUAGE = GREAT RESULTS

LANGUAGE IS CRITICAL

Language is the cornerstone of human civilization. It is unique among all forms of animal communication[4]. It binds us together. It divides us apart. It permeates every aspect of our interactions with ourselves, with each other, and with the world. It has given birth to the great literary works that have been part of our collective consciousness for thousands of years.

Sun Tsu's *The Art of War*, written in the 5th century BC, is still quoted today. Books like The Holy Bible and The Holy Qur'an have sown the seeds of both humankind's most horrific wars and its most astoundingly beautiful works of art, architecture, and humanity.

Language moves us. It inspires us. It touches us. It's… awesome.

But we aren't here to talk about all that.

LANGUAGE IS ROI

If you're reading this book right now, your interest in language and its effect on human behavior is far more acute. For you, your CFO and probably your CEO, language use is measured in the KPIs, clicks-through, audience engagement, and (most importantly) the ROI it generates. You, and thousands like you, rely upon keeping armies of copywriters shackled to their desks. But demand for copy is insatiable; there simply aren't enough good copywriters out there to create all the copy every brand needs every day. The demand for content grows by the day, and the problem gets bigger and bigger.

I remember what it was like back when I began my career in marketing. The language and marketing copy that we used was the culmination of countless meetings, endless hours of thought and discussion, and no small amount of market testing, and I'll bet your company works the same way. But guess what? Even after all that effort, without using the right technology, there's a good chance that we all get it wrong. Gut instinct can only get you so far in business, and the same is true with copywriting.

The fundamental question of branding, marketing, and advertising is, and always has been: 'what's the most effective way to deliver our message?'

And, as it turns out, the answer is the key to unlocking your brand's true marketing potential. Those brands that find the answer rise to the top of their industries and make billions. Those that don't fade into obscurity, victims of their own marketing impotence.

The question of how best to deliver a brand's message is, in many ways, the impetus for the creation of this very book. I know firsthand how hard it can be to communicate even a very valuable message. It's true! Let me explain. AI-Powered Copywriting helps brands reach and engage their audiences more effectively than they are today. But it's a strange and confusing idea for many. It is one that I have struggled to articulate from the very earliest days of AI-Powered Copywriting's genesis. This struggle dogged me as I walked, hat in hand, from one venture capital firm to another, fastidiously striving to get my unique concept off the ground. It wasn't until we nailed the messaging for Phrasee that we hit the hockey-stick of growth.

This is the crux of The Language Effect; the right copy will make you millions, and Phrasee is the proof. But the wrong language – and you'll be on the breadline.

It is my hope that this book will help you understand why marketers of the future need to understand The Language Effect – and know how to use it to their advantage.

So, let's get right into it.

MARKETING LANGUAGE: YOU CAN'T AFFORD TO GET IT WRONG

Every interaction with a brand's marketing has a real impact. And, often, it's the language contained in that marketing that determines whether that impact will turn out to be a net positive or a net negative.

Just ask Reebok, whose 2012 'Cheat on your girlfriend, not your workout' campaign ran afoul of women's rights advocates[5], or fashion brand Kenneth Cole, which tried to piggyback on the massive coverage of the 'Arab Spring' in 2011 by suggesting in a tweet that the unrest was attributable to the impending release of their spring collection[6] – your copy matters… a lot!

Using the wrong language in your marketing can have massive real-world consequences. It can alienate consumers, drive them away from your brand, and negatively affect your bottom line.

Conversely, using the **right** language in your marketing can have just the opposite effect.

If you've ever offended a spouse or parent without intending to, it was quite likely a case of 'it's not what you said, it's how you said it.' This age-old maxim isn't just relevant in the context of an upset loved one, however. In marketing, these are words to live by.

“USING THE WRONG LANGUAGE IN YOUR MARKETING CAN HAVE MASSIVE REAL-WORLD CONSEQUENCES.”

By way of an example, let's look at a young, up-and-coming startup based in Cupertino, California: Apple. Today, Steve Jobs' progeny is a trillion-dollar company[7], and according to Interbrand's Best Global Brands 2019 report[8], it's also the world's most valuable brand, at about $232 billion USD.

But things weren't always this way.

Back in 1997, Apple laid off a third of its workforce, and, as its late co-founder Steve Jobs later admitted, was 90 days away from being completely broke.

As Jack Nicas put it in a 2018 *New York Times* article, 'Apple's ascent from the brink of bankruptcy to the world's most valuable public company has been a business tour de force, marked by rapid innovation, a series of smash-hit products and the creation of a sophisticated, globe-spanning supply chain that keeps costs down while producing enormous volumes of cutting-edge devices.[9]'

Indeed, Apple's mind-boggling journey to the highest heights of tech success can be attributed in large measure to its knack for developing some of the most iconic and beloved tech products the world has ever seen. But this success story isn't simply one of innovative products and effective supply chain management; it's also a masterclass in effective branding, marketing, and, of course, nailing your marketing copy. It's a masterclass of which every brand and marketer should take heed.

Ask yourself this: what makes average computer users, for most of whom a $900 PC would be more than enough for their needs, drop $2,800 on a MacBook Pro? Ask most why they did so, and very few will be able to give you a coherent answer.

'Macs are better.' Or so, this is what a lot of people would argue. But most don't know exactly *why* they know this. It's one of the most pervasive, fascinating, and inexplicable phenomena in the history of modern branding.

Interestingly, if you line up the marketing copy Apple used leading up to its darkest days, and contrast it with that used during its meteoric rise to the top of the tech game, you can see a massive branding shift take place, even if only in the brand's slogans.

That's what separates the marketing copy that 'works' from that which doesn't. Ultimately, 'good' marketing copy elicits the response you want from your customers. In Apple's case, the desired response was for consumers to become convinced that paying more for a Mac product was worth the extra expense. The Apple brand's success hinged upon this premise.

In the end, Apple's marketing managed to accomplish exactly that, and the language the brand chose played a major role in its incredible marketing success.

That, in essence, is The Language Effect – and its impact cannot be ignored.

The evolution of Apple's marketing copy[10]

Late 70'S — "Byte into an apple"

Meh.

Early 80'S — "Soon there will be two kinds of people. Those who use computers and those who use Apples."

An effective branding approach is taking shape, but it's clunky and ineffective.

1984 — "The computer for the rest of us"

Not quite there yet.

1990 — "The power to be your best"

What the...?

1997 — "Think different"

It begins (the year Apple finally began to turn things around).

2002 — "Switch"

Now we're cooking with gas.

2006 — "Get a Mac"

A LOT of people did exactly that.

IT'S NOT WHAT YOU SAY, IT'S HOW YOU SAY IT

The underlying message of every marketing campaign is, at its core, essentially the same: 'my product exists, please buy it.' Every consumer is intrinsically aware of this immutable marketing truth.

A world filled with advertisements simply proclaiming, 'my product exists, please buy it', however, never materialized. Instead, we live in a world where that quintessential marketing message is presented to consumers in a million different, highly sophisticated forms. Instead, brands spend billions of dollars each year making sure that their marketing messages are presented to the world in the most effective, positive way possible. It isn't 'my product exists, please buy it'; it's 'Have a Coke and a smile', 'Pass the Heinz', or 'Got milk?' It's celebrity endorsements. It's beautiful people having a great time. It's advertising interruptions during your favorite TV program. It's Super Bowl commercials that cost two million bucks a minute.

This all adds up to a digital reality where the average consumer in the United States is exposed to more than 5,000 advertisements per day[11]. Cutting through all the clutter to deliver a branded message that resonates and engages has never been more difficult... or more crucial to your brand's bottom line.

Subtle differences in wording, sentence structure, punctuation and even the inclusion or exclusion of an emoji in the copy you choose can have a huge impact on how well a given ad, email, billboard, or campaign performs. Measured over several campaigns, ads, or sends, this impact snowballs into a massive difference in revenue generated.

SMALL CHANGES = BIG RESULTS

Digital marketing channels offer brands reach on a grand scale. If a brand is so inclined, it can reach tens of millions of consumers with the push of a button. With reach like that available at your fingertips, even a small incremental increase in user engagement can represent millions of dollars in extra revenue.

The fact is, the strategies and tools capable of generating incremental increases in user engagement are not only readily available, but also quite common in the digital marketing space. So how can you get ahead of the game? Brands invest billions of dollars worldwide each year in these strategies and tools. And yet, counter-intuitively, few focus their efforts (and budgets) on developing an effective, repeatable, data-based approach to writing better marketing copy. Worse yet – the vast majority leave it to the gut instinct of humans. Wow.

There are, however, many tales of language-driven success in the marketing and branding arena – what we call The

Language Effect. They span many digital marketing channels and many industries, from retail to travel to finance and beyond. Some of these you'll read about in subsequent chapters of this very book.

These stories tell an important tale. A tale that every brand and marketer needs to hear. A tale of marketing failure, marketing success, and the power of The Language Effect. It's a tale that needs to be told.

HOW DID COPYWRITING GET LEFT BEHIND?

On the internet, and on phones, and even on watches, the language you use is critical. It conveys your message. It is the foundation upon which any marketing message is built. Now, of course, investing in top-notch images/video for your digital marketing is important. They say that a picture says a thousand words, after all, and more than a few advertising agencies around the world will gladly take your money to produce a snazzy video or photoshop a killer graphic. But – and it's a big BUT – if the copy is ineffective, then it's all a big, fat waste of time and money. People get so caught up in the fancy stuff, they forget the basics.

Think about it. When you go to Google and search for something – the results are given in text. When you go to a product website, there are pictures – and then language that drives you through your purchase process. And in email marketing – from the subject line through to the body content – images are peripheral, and what you write is the crux of all your efforts.

In the endless battle to engage the modern digital audience, the copy brands use to communicate with their audiences has been overlooked for far too long.

Copywriting is the forgotten child of digital marketing – left to wallow in relative obscurity, while the market's heads are turned by complicated (and expensive) solutions to digital marketing problems that provide a fraction of the impact.

But as you'll see, copywriting – and The Language Effect – shouldn't be relegated to the minor leagues. It's a major league problem... and, more importantly, a major league opportunity.

2

FORGET WHAT YOU THOUGHT YOU KNEW ABOUT MARKETING COPY

THE BAD NEWS, AND THE GOOD

I've got some bad news for you: there is no 'secret sauce' when it comes to marketing copy. The days of shortcuts to better copy performance are done. The spammy clickbait tactics of yesteryear simply don't cut it in our new digitally driven reality. Tricking your audience into engaging with your marketing through spurious copywriting strategies will get you nowhere (or at least, not for long).

Differentiating your brand from everyone else's is the key to standing out in the digital marketing arena, and standing out is the key to success. It would be great if things were as simple as 'Use these words or phrases in your marketing and you'll make a whole bunch of extra money'. But that's not how marketing works. In the real world, audience tastes, and marketing copy effectiveness, can change on a dime, and what works today might not work tomorrow.

But I've also got some good news for you! The power of your brand's voice to affect consumer perception is quite simply unparalleled.

Here's the catch: in a digital age where marketing channels abound, and quality marketing copy is at a premium (and scarce), a great slogan simply doesn't cut it anymore.

It takes mountains of marketing to have an impact. Audiences have migrated from traditional channels (like television, radio, and print) to digital platforms (like social networks, streaming services, search, and email) in massive numbers. This migration will accelerate in the months and years to come.

Straddling the line between i) standing out from the crowd, ii) staying on brand, and iii) engaging audiences without resorting to cheap tricks has never been more crucial.

Old ways of thinking about marketing copy simply aren't going to work when it comes to your brand making an impact today. Let me show you the new way…

IS YOUR COPY HELPING YOUR BRAND STAND OUT?

> **'Phrasee delivers a solution that helps ensure we stand out in a crowded market.'**
>
> *Tom Lowe, Head of Subscription Trading, The Times*

In a large-scale split test, my Phrasee team applied sound scientific methodology to one of marketing's most enduring tropes: building holiday-specific campaigns for significant days on the marketing calendar – such as Christmas and Black Friday.

What kind of impact, we wondered, does including the words 'Black Friday' or 'Christmas' in a subject line actually have on that campaign's marketing performance?

It depends, as it turns out.

We ran the stats on thousands of email subject line split tests, and the results are perplexing. Campaigns that used Black Friday-specific copy in their subject lines generated lower open rates in over 40% of cases. Does that surprise you? It means that using only Black Friday-specific copy in the subject lines could be costing you valuable audience engagement more than 40% of the time. It also means that using the words 'Black Friday' worked less than 60% of the time, so it's basically a coin flip. Not very conclusive, is it?

But that's not all, when it comes to Christmas email marketing campaigns, the results are even more perplexing. In a full 55% of cases, campaigns which used non-Christmas-specific copy in their email subject lines generated more opens.

Data like this should make every brand and marketer rethink the way they approach and execute marketing copy. It also raises a few very important questions:

- If including the words 'Christmas' or 'Black Friday' in the language that brands use for their Christmas and Black Friday campaigns can have a negative impact about half the time, why do so many brands use it all the time?
- If everyone else is including the words 'Black Friday' and 'Christmas' in their campaigns, and standing out in a crowded digital world is such a high priority, might it not make more sense to try doing something different with your brand's Christmas and Black Friday campaign copy?
- What should your brand do instead?

Sadly, there are no easy answers. Following Apple's lead and using better copy in your brand's marketing takes work, effort, and no small amount of rigor.

YOUR BRAND IS UNIQUE... BUT IS YOUR COPY?

The truth is, the answer to the question, 'What makes marketing copy work?' will be completely different for your brand than it was for Apple. Why? Two reasons: first, because your brand's marketing goals are almost certainly different from those of Apple; second, because the tastes and preferences of your brand's and Apple's audience are almost certainly different.

Every brand is different. Every audience is different. Every relationship between brand and consumer is different. Learning about and embracing these important differences are the keys to unlocking the benefits of The Language Effect.

HOW TO GET THE EDGE

There is NO secret sauce to getting effective marketing copy at scale. There is, however, a repeatable roadmap to optimized marketing copy. As you'll see, building a better copywriting strategy for your brand requires you to look at it from an entirely new angle.

There are, however, a few universal pitfalls that every brand should avoid. These pitfalls apply across every industry, every audience, and every brand. Eliminating the strategies that consistently make marketing copy fail – that negatively impact consumer perceptions of your brand, and that damage the crucial relationships you've built with your customers – is where you need to start your quest toward more effective marketing copy. This is what we'll be exploring in the next chapter.

Visit **thelanguageeffect.com** for more information about our analysis of Black Friday email campaigns and subject line performance.

3

WHAT MAKES MARKETING LANGUAGE FAIL?

AN UNDESERVED LESSON

When I was working in Amsterdam in 2009, my company ran huge trade shows – including an immense one in Frankfurt, Germany (as an aside, it is an inarguable fact that Germans LOVE trade shows). While we were by far the market leaders in our industry, there were tangential sectors that were underserved.

So, I went away and wrote what I thought was a killer message, to be used across email, web and direct mail. We got it designed and sent off to hundreds of thousands of people – including my CEO Simon.

Simon was a dichotomous character. Mild-mannered and numbers-driven by day, you put him in front of a Manchester United game by night and the language even made me blush (and my vocabulary is one step up from that of a sailor!). When Simon got riled, you shut up, and you listened.

Anyway, he was on a secret seed list[12] for our marketing and got the materials. He called me into his office, and things started off with Angelic Simon. He asked me if I had signed off the content, and of course, I proudly stood by my work!

But then, as if a switch was flicked, Devil Simon came out. And Devil Simon taught me something about language that I'll never forget.

His bugbear was the strapline: 'the show for underserved markets.'

Sounds fine, right? After all, it was a trade show designed for underserved markets. Boxes were ticked! But it wasn't fine. Devil Simon had come up as a marketer, and he knew a thing or two about language. Devil Simon made a totally valid point, albeit with a few more expletives than I can include here. His point was that a lot of people will read 'underserved' as 'undeserved'. And by mentally swapping the order of just a couple letters, the entire meaning of the value proposition would be misinterpreted by a huge swathe of our audience.

At first, I thought he was overreacting. I thought I was 'undeserving' of his feedback. I indignantly went back to my desk and stewed for what seemed like hours.

Then Simon's lesson hit me; I had been thinking about language totally wrong all these years.

It doesn't matter how you want people to interpret your message. What does matter is how they actually interpret it. And since that day, I've made it my life's mission to never underserve undeserving audiences (did I get that right?).

WHAT DOES FAILURE LOOK LIKE?

But before we can talk about what makes marketing copy fail, it is important to define exactly what 'fail' looks like. If marketing copy that 'works' drives audience engagement, builds robust brand-consumer relationships, and ultimately elicits the types of responses you want from your audience, marketing copy that 'fails' accomplishes exactly the opposite. Worse still, if your copy generates a strong negative response in the form of audience feedback, the debate over whether or not your marketing copy has failed is officially over. It has failed, big time. Negative interactions with a brand's marketing copy alienate audiences. It makes your brand a nuisance. It results in unsubscribes and 'I don't want to see this' complaints on Facebook ads.

It lands your emails in the dreaded spam folder. In the end, it negatively impacts your brand's bottom line.

There are lots of ways your language will fail. Here are a few of the most common offenders.

1 – YOU GET THE CONTEXT WRONG

During her tenure as Digital Marketing Manager at music technology company MakeMusic, wunderkind Kait Creamer spent most of early 2018 having chats with MakeMusic's data and engineering teams about what the company might need to do to handle the EU's impending General Data Protection Regulation (GDPR) legislation effectively.

The MakeMusic team decided that since the brand had such a small international audience, they could safely opt EU subscribers out of emails without much impact to their business. Thus, an opt-in email built specifically for MakeMusic's EU-based audience was deemed unnecessary.

As is so often the case with such things, the team at MakeMusic ended up sending a last-minute opt-in message after all. Kait decided that, in her words, 'If I was going to have to be one of those marketers sending GDPR bullsh*t, I might as well try to make the email engaging and helpful[13].'

Because the email being sent was destined for subscribers to SmartMusic (one of MakeMusic's brands), and SmartMusic's most-loved repertoire was its Star Wars suite, Kait figured that May the 4th[14] would be the perfect opportunity to send the GDPR email (which makes a lot of sense, if you think about it!). The Star Wars-themed email included links to Star Wars-related recordings, Darth Vader imagery, Star Wars puns, et cetera. In addition, Kait also segmented the message so that those who regularly opened and engaged with the brand's emails got a slightly different version than those who hadn't opened in a while.

Once the campaign was built and ready to go, all that remained was to write email subject lines for each of Kait's audience segments. In her search for inspiration, Kait stumbled upon a Phrasee blog post entitled *8 Awesome May the 4th Subject Lines No-one has used yet.* The post was one of a series of parody posts[15], human-written by design (and also absurd), and they centered around silly subject lines for significant events in the yearly email marketing campaign calendar (Christmas, Black Friday, International Pizza Day etc.).

One of the hilariously human subject lines included in the post was 'I find your lack of opened emails disturbing', a play on a Darth Vader quote from *Star Wars, Episode IV: A New Hope*[16]. Kait said this particular subject line made her laugh out loud. She figured it was perfect for her campaign. It was (again in her own words): 'cheeky, funny, and super crazy relevant'. Kait ran it by a bunch of folks on her team, who all thought it was a great subject line, and then she sent the campaign.

Here's what Kait said happened next:

> 'As it turns out, a bunch of people DO NOT know or appreciate Star Wars references that sound like an angry email marketer's trying to call them out on their lack of engagement. I got a bunch of really rude responses, sent personal apologies to about a dozen folks (who says I'm not a people pleaser?!), then gave up and called it a day. Lesson learned: don't assume people have the same context, background, or perspective you do. Just because you and your co-workers think something is good or funny, that doesn't mean your audience will.
>
> 'Though, TBH, the whole incident is really funny in retrospect. C'est la vie.'

C'est la vie indeed.

On just the right audience, and under just the right circumstances, Kait's 'I find your lack of opened emails disturbing' email subject line could've performed exceedingly well. Kait's assumption – that most of the audience segment she was trying to engage would get the joke because her data said that MakeMusic's Star Wars suite was highly popular with that audience – was, on its surface, a sound one.

However, negative audience feedback taught Kait a valuable lesson about marketing copy in the digital age – a lesson which has been borne out by the performance data of millions of marketing campaigns all across the globe: when it comes to marketing copy, context is everything.

2 – YOUR INTENTION IS NOT INTERPRETED AS YOU INTENDED

Before I got a bollocking[17] from Devil Simon for talking about underserved markets, and before Kait inadvertently offended Star Wars neophytes, I hadn't understood a critical dynamic in every human interaction: intent vs. interpretation.

As a wise monk and poet named John Lydgate famously said way back in the 15th century, 'You can please some of the people all of the time, you can please all of the people some of the time, but you can't please all of the people all of the time.[18]' Although John Lydgate wasn't referring to marketing copy, he might as well have been.

While pleasing all the people all the time with your brand's marketing copy is indeed a laudable goal, it's important to be realistic.

“WHEN IT COMES TO MARKETING COPY, CONTEXT IS EVERYTHING.”

I've used marketing copy that didn't resonate with my audience – and chances are you and your team have too. But this isn't just down to us – it's down to our audience, and the contextual frame through which they interpret what you've written. It's sort of like the platitudes you're told after getting dumped by your squeeze: it's not you, it's them.

HOW CAN YOU GET IT RIGHT WHEN THE GOALPOSTS ARE CONSTANTLY MOVING?

Optimizing your marketing copy for the abstract 'them' is an infinitely complex marketing problem to solve. 'They' are a diverse, fickle bunch, each with their own histories, tastes, preferences, hopes, dreams, and needs. 'Their' tastes change by the year, the month, the week, and even the day.

Your audience's perceptions of your marketing copy, and your brand, will be impacted by myriad factors, many entirely beyond your control.

Think about it like this. Let's say one day after work you go home, have a nice filet of salmon, some broccoli and some rice, drink plenty of water, and are in bed by 10pm. You get a full eight hours' sleep and wake up ready to tackle the day.

Or maybe you go for a 'quick one after work' with your co-workers in the local boozer. A quick 'one' turns into 12 pints of gassy lager. You somehow make it home, although you have no idea how, and wake up after five hours of broken sleep with a half-eaten kebab on your chest, your mind in a haze, wondering what happened last night.

Now let's say you get an email. You're going to respond to it differently based upon your context, be it salmon or kebab. But: there isn't a personalization system on the planet that could have predicted your context on the morning in question!

And yet all you seem to read about these days is the latest and greatest personalization techniques. Billions of dollars have been spent on building personalization tools, and, according to thousands of tech companies offering personalization solutions, it is the most important thing ever. But it's not – because if the copy you use sucks, then all the personalization in the world is a big old waste of time.

Technology has been used to disrupt nearly every part of the marketing mix... except one: copywriting. Why? Because it was too hard a problem to solve.

But it's a problem that is costing you millions of dollars.

4

WHAT IS NON-OPTIMIZED MARKETING COPY COSTING YOU RIGHT NOW?

WHERE'S THE BEEF?

Way back in 1984, fast-food mega-chain Burger King launched one of the most successful viral marketing campaigns of all time. The slogan of that campaign? *'Where's the beef?'*

The campaign was built around a TV ad featuring three elderly ladies lifting the top off the comically large hamburger they had just purchased. Inside was an equally comically tiny burger patty. They were understandably annoyed.

In subsequent television ads, the three women complained about the lack of beef in their burgers wherever they could. They called an executive from the company that sold them the burger on his yacht, yelling, 'Where's the beef?' into the receiver until he fell out of his deck chair. They yelled through the brand's drive-thru windows at the presumably terrified employees inside.

In every case, the phrase remained the same: 'Where's the beef?' Its catchy tagline out of the way, the ads got to the point. A narrator explained that Burger King's burgers contained more beef than its closest competitor, McDonald's. The campaign's underlying message was clear.

The campaign and its tagline went on to become a cultural phenomenon across America. Presidential candidate Walter Mondale actually said, 'Where's the beef?' during a presidential debate! The phrase appeared on bumper stickers. It was mentioned on a slew of television shows. It even wound up as a Milton Bradley board game[19].

'Where's the beef?' took on a life of its own. But, as the phrase spread through the common consciousness, its connection to the Burger King brand quickly faded.

Need proof? The 'Where's the beef?' campaign wasn't actually developed by Burger King at all. It was launched by rival fast-food chain Wendy's. You may have remembered that, but unfortunately for Wendy's, the majority of people didn't know which brand had come up with the strapline.

Over time, Wendy's didn't reap the benefits of the phrase's ubiquity.

Considering the viral (was it even possible to 'go viral' in 1984?) reaction to the 'Where's the beef?' campaign, the sales and branding potential for Wendy's was absolutely massive. Due to factors beyond Wendy's control, however, a huge increase in sales off the back of a wildly successful marketing campaign simply never materialized. Indeed, by 1985, Wendy's executives presumably wondered to themselves where the beef was.

Does this mean that 'Where's the beef?' was poor marketing language? Certainly not. It was a finely crafted campaign that connected with consumers in a way that few could've predicted. Equally few, however, could have predicted the phrase's gradual diversion from the brand it was supposed to promote. 'Where's the beef?' succeeded, just not for Wendy's.

That's the thing with marketing language: the 'why' is just as important as the 'how', if not more so.

You write with a specific goal in mind. That goal might be brand awareness (views), or audience engagement (likes, shares, follows). Maybe it's conversions (subscriptions, signups), or perhaps it's attributable sales. Every minute and every cent you spend writing and distributing marketing that doesn't directly line up with your goals will amount to nothing more than a black hole in your budget.

“THAT’S THE THING WITH MARKETING LANGUAGE: THE ‘WHY’ IS JUST AS IMPORTANT AS THE ‘HOW’.”

QUANTIFYING THE LANGUAGE EFFECT (WITH AN UNNECESSARILY COMPLEX FORMULA)

The ultimate goal of marketing is to increase revenue. It always has been, and it always will be. Marketing goals like brand awareness, audience engagement, and conversions are ultimately proxies for your overarching goal.

Quantifying the increase in revenue due to The Language Effect is no simple matter. When asked to explain how it was done for the purposes of this book, Phrasee co-founder and chief scientist, Dr. Neil Yager, produced something that looked a bit like this:

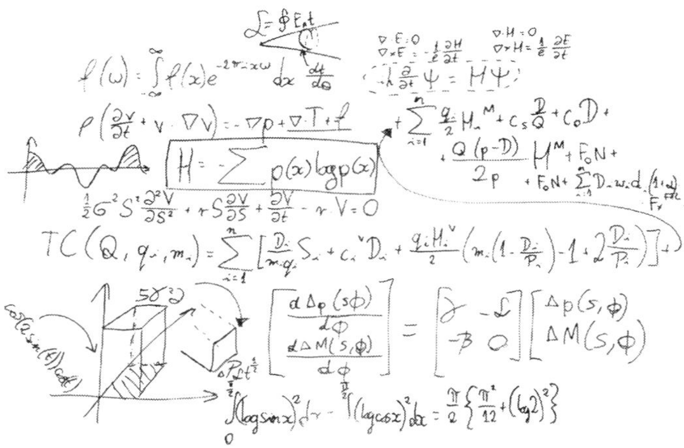

An unnecessarily complicated mathematical formula[20]

Confused? So was I. Fortunately, there's a much easier way to estimate the cost of using non-optimized language in your marketing copy. Using email subject lines as an example, it looks like this:

(audience size) x (open rate non-optimized – open rate optimized) x (conversion rate) x (average order value) = (revenue lost)

Here's an example.

Let's say that you're a retail brand with 1,000,000 subscribers on your list.

We'll assume that the open rate generated by a subject line built with optimized copy is 13%, while without it's 11%.

This 2% difference in open rate might not sound like much, but it can have a very real (and quite significant) impact on an email marketing campaign's bottom line.

An open rate difference of just 2% leads to 20,000 fewer opens per campaign.

Multiply those 20,000 extra opens by the campaign's conversion rate (let's say 1%).

20,000 X conversion rate [1%] = 200 fewer conversions from using non-optimized email subject line language.

Now multiply those 200 extra conversions by your brand's average order value (let's say $50).

Extra conversions [200] X average order value [$50] = $10,000

1,000,000 x (0.13-0.11) x 0.01 x 50 = $10,000

Using non-optimized language in your campaign's email subject line has just cost your retail brand $10,000 in potential revenue from a single email marketing campaign. And that's just one email send. Extrapolate that across all your social ads, push messages, search ads, your website and the like – and you're leaving millions of dollars on the table.

This kind of back-of-the-envelope calculation, while over-simplified for the sake of brevity, illustrates an important point: finding ways to boost performance at any stage of the buying journey (even by a small amount) has a very real effect on your bottom line.

The Language Effect moves the performance needle for digital marketing's most important metrics.

Even if the differences between optimized copy and non-optimized copy may not be immediately obvious to the naked eye, they matter.

Let's look at an example.

Daily deals brand Wowcher was looking to optimize their Facebook ad campaigns. They had a very specific marketing problem to solve: how to generate more leads. There is no question that there are leads to be found on Facebook; with 2.7 billion users worldwide, it has become one of the world's most important marketing channels. But as more than 6 million businesses[21] now advertise on the platform, capturing user attention and generating leads through Facebook advertising isn't easy.

Sure, Wowcher's Facebook ads were generating leads, but not enough of them. Furthermore, the cost of generating each lead was too high, and had been for some time. Whether Facebook would remain a crucial channel for Wowcher was not in doubt. The question, instead, was: could better ad copy bring better results? (Spoiler alert: the answer is yes.)

The team at Wowcher decided to run some tests to see how better copy would impact Facebook ad performance. Every element of Wowcher's Facebook ads – from the images to the audience segments the ads reached – were identical. The only variable in the tests was the marketing language itself.

In these large-scale tests, the ads built with optimized copy reduced cost per lead (CPL) by 31.2%. For a brand like Wowcher, who run Facebook ad campaigns on a large scale, such a decrease in CPL represents a huge increase in marketing efficiency, and ultimately revenue. They now understand The Language Effect.

Wowcher certainly isn't alone here, both in terms of benefiting from The Language Effect, and using AI-Powered Copywriting to get there. Hundreds of businesses across the globe – from retail brands to airlines to banks and all points in between – have begun experimenting with Phrasee's AI-Powered Copywriting across dozens of channels. And, in almost every case, the results have been similarly impressive.

In the quest to optimize their digital marketing campaigns, many brands and marketers have overlooked something of crucial importance: The Language Effect. The construction of a campaign's copy often means the difference between success and failure. But, as discussed, there aren't enough human copywriters to go around. And even if there were, their biases hold them back.

So what can you do? The answer isn't human intelligence. The answer is artificial intelligence – or, more specifically, AI-Powered Copywriting.

Read more on this case study and others at:
thelanguageeffect.com

5

IF IT'S SO HARD, WHY IS THERE NO TECH TO HELP?

WHY TECH GOT A BAD RAP

The quest to connect with consumers has taken brands down some pretty dark paths of late.

Big Tech's relaxed attitude toward user data opened the door for some extremely concerning marketing behavior. The Cambridge Analytica scandal[22] was just the tip of the iceberg. Legitimate questions about how exactly consumer data is being collected, and what exactly it's being used for, make headlines every day. The battle between the relevance, targeting, and engagement needs of brands and the privacy concerns of consumers has only just begun.

The opening shots – in the form of shady industry tactics and bold new legislation like the much-lauded General Data Protection Regulation (GDPR)[23] – have already been fired. Few, however, can tell where all of this is headed.

Within this context, consumer expectations are shifting, and the digital user experience is evolving. This presents both brands and marketers with new customer experience challenges to overcome by the day. Today's consumer expects you to deliver a personalized, relevant marketing experience. But, it seems, they are reluctant to provide you with the data and insights required to deliver that experience at scale.

THE MARTECH EXPLOSION

This dichotomy has created the perfect conditions for innovative new technologies to enter the marketing arena.

And enter it they have.

Every year, Chiefmartec puts out a marketing technology (martech) landscape – the marketing technology world's definitive list of brands operating in the martech space – and every year, it gets bigger. You know the chart I'm talking about. But what began as a fascinating mosaic of technological progress has become a flummoxing Jackson Pollock-esque tornado of chaos – and has outlived its usefulness.

“

TODAY’S CONSUMER EXPECTS YOU TO DELIVER A PERSONALIZED, RELEVANT MARKETING EXPERIENCE.

”

Automation platforms keep drip campaigns cycling into subscribers' inboxes through every stage of the buyer journey. Machine learning algorithms, written by researchers with PhDs in astrophysics, make useful recommendations on precisely where and when digital banner ads should appear on a given marketing channel. In some cases, these AI marketing applications even purchase ad placements on their own. Targeting and retargeting tools deliver relevant digital content to the right user in the right place at the right time with increasing precision.

But what about your language?

Amid all the relevance, targeting, and data analytics hubbub, it seems that marketing copywriting has been forgotten, abandoned in the never-ending pursuit of more and more data.

But why is this? Why has the crux of all your marketing – the language you use – been ignored?

TIMES HAVE CHANGED

'Right person, right ad, right time' has long been digital marketing's Holy Grail. That perfect combination of ad design and delivery that leaves the consumer all but powerless to resist your brand's considerable charms. It makes sense that almost every aspect of marketing and advertising has been touched by advanced technology in some form or another.

But something is missing.

Once you've built up your martech stack and perfected the art of getting your brand's message exactly where it needs to be, exactly when it needs to be there, quite an obvious question emerges:

What should that message be?

Finding an effective data-driven approach to answering this question, as it turns out, is a hard problem. A very hard problem. And that's why so few have dared to tackle it.

Personally, I love a hard problem, which is probably why I decided to make this one my own.

Copywriting is the last marketing discipline to be touched by advanced technology. This is quite an odd truth, considering copywriting possesses the potential to generate the highest ROI of the bunch.

The reason behind this is simple: using AI to complete a task that's so uniquely human is a very complex problem, both in terms of the technical approach and the philosophy underpinning it.

See, determining the best day and time to post a Facebook ad, or which of your customers recently abandoned their digital shopping cart and are due for a retargeting ad to close the sale, are far simpler problems to solve. As such, these problems require relatively simple tools to solve them at scale. And that's why there are a million and one vendors who will gleefully take your money.

Copywriting – both the writing of it and the predicting of how specific language will perform on a brand's unique audience – is a different matter altogether. With few proven technological solutions available, copywriting has been left to the intuitive whims and 'gut feel' of legions of copywriters.

In many cases, these copywriters are extremely talented people. They've built successful careers out of knowing just what to say to a brand's audience and just how to say it. That's why a good copywriter has always been, and always will be, such a valuable resource for any brand.

Copywriters have delivered the most iconic and effective slogans, taglines, and campaigns in the history of marketing. They've brought brands from relative obscurity to the forefront of their industries with little more than a single line of catchy, engaging text. They are a crucial part of any effective marketing strategy.

But times have changed.

The emergence of digital marketing channels has turned the world of copywriting on its head. The battle for consumer attention has veered onto strange new paths.

This isn't the first time in technological history that 'strange new paths' have come into play, however.

At some point in our history, humanity's increasingly complex mathematical understanding and need for scalable calculations gave birth to the abacus (and eventually the calculator). Growing demand for printed copy brought forth the printing press. Increased consumer demand for motor vehicles led to the perfecting of the assembly line.

Counting by hand, copying by hand, and building a car by hand all proved to be terribly inefficient. Relying upon humans to do it was cumbersome and prone to error.

A similar monumental shift is taking place in copywriting right now – a shift in its infancy. And, whether you're ready to accept it or not, this shift is irreversible.

Relying upon the gut feeling of copywriters is inefficient.

Copywriting needs a new approach, because the old one is broken.

It demands an approach grounded in data-based reasoning and coherent strategic goals.

Let's take a look at why.

PART 2

WHY YOU NEED TO THROW OUT THE OLD RULE BOOK

'Early man walked away as modern man took control

Their minds weren't all the same, to conquer was his goal'

We're Only Gonna Die (From Our Own Arrogance)
Bad Religion

6

THE TRADITIONAL APPROACH SUCKS, AND HERE'S WHY

THE BYGONE ERA OF DON DRAPER

Picture the scene:

Don Draper stands before two executives from the HJ Heinz Company in a well-fitted, freshly pressed suit. Beside him are three posters, each mounted upon a wooden easel. On one poster is a close-up image of a hamburger. On another, some French fries. And on the last, a piece of steak on the end of a fork.

He begins his pitch...

'It's clean, it's simple, and it's tantalizingly incomplete. What's missing? One thing.'

He coolly flips a clear overlay onto each image before reading aloud the single line of text written on it. 'Pass the Heinz'.

'You mean the Heinz ketchup,' one of the executives says.

'It's Heinz,' Don Draper replies without missing a beat. 'It only means one thing.'

'It feels like half an ad,' says the executive. Clearly, he doesn't get it.

Undaunted, Draper continues… 'The greatest thing you have working for you is not the photo you take or the picture you paint, it's the imagination of the consumer. They have no budget. They have no time limit. And if you can get into that space, your ad can run all day.[24]'

Eyebrows raise throughout the room.

What a campaign! What a pitch!

What a guy.

And… scene.

For decades, this is how the advertising and marketing industry was run – massive campaigns based on one simple idea, and one line of text. Back then, folks like Don Draper were rock stars. The ad men of Madison Avenue broadcast their bold, finely crafted nuggets of marketing campaign gold to the world.

What a time to be alive!

Back in Madison Avenue's heyday, there were a limited number of channels that brands could use to market their products and services to the masses.

Print, outdoor, television, radio, point-of-sale... the list was short.

Every consumer would get essentially the same message, so it *had* to be great. There were no scientific mechanisms for testing marketing at scale[25], so gut feeling and intuition were the only guides to building a successful campaign. That's why the Don Draper types were so effective. Brands believed in these intrepid marketing pioneers. Why? Because said pioneers' instincts were better than everyone else's.

Back then, the demand for copy wasn't high, so a small number of Don Drapers were able to service the market's needs. Sure, such folks were exceedingly expensive, but with often only a single line of copy broadcasting your brand's message to the world, they were worth the investment.

Enter: the internet.

Now, you need copy for email. You also need copy for Facebook and Instagram. Don't forget about your mobile app pushes, or your website, or Twitter and WeChat. And, of course, you've got Google AdWords, display ads, and YouTube pre-rolls. Plus, what about Snapchat, TikTok, or whatever those damn kids come up with next[26]?

Today, advertising and marketing channels abound. A massive global shift away from the traditional media channels of yesteryear and toward the new digital reality is a foregone conclusion. On top of this, we've watched automation, audience segmentation, retargeting and the like forever change the ways and means by which brands reach consumers.

DON DRAPER WAS A SOLDIER. THESE DAYS YOU NEED AN ARMY

The scale of marketing copy required has now surpassed the copywriting industry's capability to meet that demand.

Think about it. In 2005, Google Ads were nascent. Facebook was a niche market. Twitter didn't even exist. The majority of consumers didn't have a smartphone. Email was not anywhere near as pervasive as it is now.

Back then, you didn't need much copy to get your message out everywhere. But fast-forward to today – and the amount of copy you need to run even the simplest marketing campaign has increased tenfold.

Therein lies a fundamental problem: there simply aren't enough qualified and talented copywriters around to satisfy the exponentially increased demand.

Brands now have many new digital marketing channels to service, none of which existed when Don Draper was pitching to Heinz. Each of these channels functions slightly differently. The audience on each channel has its own expectations, preferences, and patterns of behavior when interacting with your marketing.

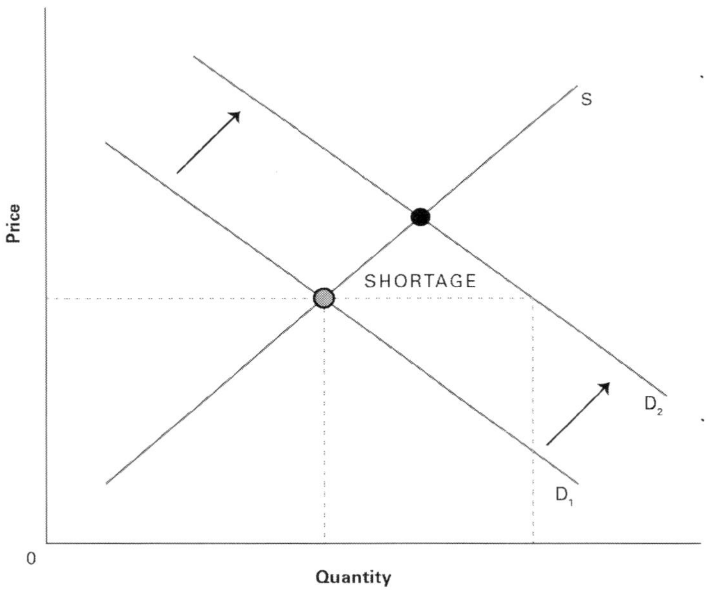

The copywriting disequilibrium

Only a decade or two ago, the supply of copywriting matched the demand (the gray dot on the above graph).

With the boom in marketing across email, Facebook, SMS, Instagram, websites, AdWords etc., global demand for copy has increased and continues to increase by the day.

“THERE SIMPLY AREN’T ENOUGH QUALIFIED AND TALENTED COPYWRITERS AROUND...”

For you economists out there, this surplus of demand and shortage of copy is represented on the graph with the demand curve shifting from D1 to D2. For those of you who need an Econ 101 refresher, think about it like this. In a normal market, when demand increases, but supply remains constant, the price goes up because the item is now more scarce. The only way to reduce that price is to increase the supply.

However – in the copywriting market, increasing the supply simply isn't possible. You can't magically invent thousands of new, talented copywriters. It's not simply a case of building a new assembly line. A thousand monkeys on a thousand typewriters, while incredibly cute to visualize, is not the solution to the marketing industry's single biggest problem.

And so now, we find ourselves in a perpetual and untenable state of disequilibrium. There are not enough talented copywriters available to satisfy the increased demand. Since you can't magically produce new, good copywriters, many marketers have compensated. Instead of focusing on the high quality of copy, they've focused on high quantity. This has resulted in the spammy, generic language that permeates the internet... and was the starting gun to the clickbait race to the bottom. Forget your brand's voice. Forget your brand's value. Hell, forget your brand, just bombard them. Gross.

The question is: with so many brands vying for the same consumer eyeballs in a crowded digital marketplace, and with quality content at a scarce premium, how can the copywriting industry rise up to meet this very real ever-growing need? Can the current copywriting paradigm deliver?

Let's take a look…

THE OLD RULE BOOK IS NO LONGER RELEVANT

Take a look at this list of actual email subject lines used by Virgin Holidays in a recent re-engagement campaign:

1. Reserved for you: it's time to book your break!
2. Is the USA calling your name?
3. 💼 To the airport – your throne is ready: 💺
4. NYC or Vegas? Boston or Miami? There's a city for everyone
5. 😍 WOW!!! Discover the scene in the USA…
6. *This* is how you city.
7. City break? Oh hello, USA ✋
8. 🏙 Got big city dreams?
9. Iconic streets and shopping on repeat
10. So many cities ✈️ 🏙 so little time…

Picture one of the copywriters on your team presenting this list to you before the launch of a campaign. She tells you that #3 on this list is the subject line that should be used for this campaign over all the others on the list. She makes her case for subject line #3 as follows:

> 'Recent campaigns including more than one emoji have generated higher click-through rates. Our audience also typically responds well to humorous language. The well-disguised call to action within the language is also a bonus here.'

Satisfied, she leaves the room. In walks another copywriter. He tells you that the previous copywriter was wrong. It is, in fact, subject line #8 that should be used.

He explains his logic:

> 'We need to appeal to our audience's whimsical perceptions of travel. This subject line does exactly that. I've also seen that subject lines phrased as a question generate more engagement than those which aren't.'

Both copywriters present a compelling case. Both are respected members of your copywriting team. You weigh up the evidence carefully, then reach your verdict. It's time to launch that campaign!

Here's the thing. Phrasee split tested all of the email subject lines on the list above in a randomized controlled experiment. The data showed that subject line #4 was actually the highest performing of the bunch in terms of actual opens and clicks through. Here's my theory as to why:

> 'While mentioning specific cities (Miami, NYC, Vegas, and Boston) in an email sent to the whole list may appear on the surface to limit the potential demographics who will engage with this subject line, as those who had been considering other cities may not bother opening it, we found that those who are interested in traveling to these particular cities are far more likely to open the email. Targeting this specific group within the travel brand's general audience produced better results than more general language, because those in the market for travel on a given day generally have some specific potential destinations in mind.'

In retrospect, it makes a lot of sense, doesn't it? While both copywriters were able to present compelling reasons for using the copy they chose, both were wrong, and your campaign performance would've suffered no matter which one you'd listened to. The best subject line option was staring you in the face the whole time, and you didn't even know it.

But… surprise! Even I was wrong! Subject line #4 wasn't the best either. Nope! #4 wasn't the best performer at all. And yet – the case above was pretty compelling, wasn't it?

See, you could probably present a reasonable case for why any of the lines on our list were the best available option. And with a good enough argument and a healthy dose of conviction, you'd be pretty persuasive.

But there's a good chance you'd be wrong. That's the thing with marketing copy: there are a *lot* of variables at play. Finding just the right way to say something can be a tough task!

In case you were wondering, the highest-performing email subject line on this list was actually #1**.** Why? Who knows, but the data doesn't lie – #1 was the highest performer by a statistically significant margin in Virgin Holiday's multivariate test.

The reasons your audience chooses to open or ignore your brand's marketing email are complex and varied. Far too complex and varied to bother yourself (or your copywriters) with.

There is no 'secret sauce'. Well, maybe there is, and maybe Don Draper could explain it to you. But he's not here, and he's not in your office either. And if he were here, asking him to use his considerable talents to write email subject lines, or Facebook ads, or copy buried on page 1000 of your website, would probably be a massive waste of an incredibly valuable resource, don't you think?

> **'Phrasee's AI has increased our email revenue by a few million pounds! Calling Phrasee's product "awesome" doesn't quite do it justice!'**
>
> ***Saul Lopes,***
> ***Customer Lifecycle Lead (former), Virgin Holidays***

WE NEED A NEW RULE BOOK

The year is 1988. A dozen eggs cost 79 cents[27]. *Who Framed Roger Rabbit* is the year's biggest Hollywood blockbuster, and Bobby McFerrin's 'Don't Worry, Be Happy' dominates the airwaves.

Meanwhile, at The University of Michigan, PhD student, John Knoll is hard at work putting the finishing touches on a program on his Macintosh Plus that allows him to display greyscale images on a monochrome display. His program went on to become known as Photoshop, and it changed the photo editing business forever.

Pre-Photoshop, photo editing was a complex, time-consuming process. Each photograph had to be retouched by hand, using paint or ink, or pieced together in a darkroom using separate photographs[28].

As the scale and scope of the advertising business grew, the sophistication of its methods grew more complex. Armies of photo editors emerged, and darkrooms proliferated. Gradually, the market's need for images began to outstrip the photo editing industry's capacity to supply them.

When a practical application of Knoll's Photoshop program became widely available, it sold like hotcakes. Sure, there were skeptics and purists who believed the old way was superior. And yes, many photo editors feared that these emerging digital photo editing tools could soon put them out of work. Few could argue, however, that this wasn't a tool that the industry desperately needed.

As they added this powerful new digital tool to their skillsets, few photo editors were actually put out of work. In fact, the ability to edit photos without the need of a darkroom coupled with the emergence of the internet, and today's demand for marketing visuals has created a greater need for photo editors than ever before. On top of this, the quality of work the industry is now able to produce has increased dramatically.

Can you see the parallels?

We stand at the precipice of a similar shift in the way marketing copy is written. Digital technologies and the internet have created a new marketing paradigm. Reaching an audience in the digital age has become a complicated proposition.

The scales at which brands and advertisers need images requires tools like Photoshop. Nobody has a darkroom anymore. Digital photo editing tools have become a basic necessity across almost every sector of the business, and they've made marketing imagery better than ever.

The truth is the advertising/marketing industry's need for quality copy isn't far behind that of imagery. To give you an idea of the scale of the problem, over 100 billion emails are sent by businesses around the world each day[29], and 6 million global businesses are currently advertising on Facebook[30].

The thing is, to make the most of the plethora of advertising options these days, you need not just a high quantity of copy, but a high quality of copy. That is, optimized copy. A *lot* of optimized copy. So, where's that copy going to come from?

As we've established, the Don Draper model simply isn't scalable. It would require a veritable army of above-average copywriters, ready and willing to supply every brand and advertising firm with mountains of top-notch copy. Unfortunately, that simply isn't an achievable outcome.

The copywriting industry is in need of a powerful Photoshop-esque tool of its own. Simply throwing more and more humans at this growing problem is never going to work – because there aren't enough qualified humans out there.

So why is it humans are lackluster at picking good copy? Two reasons. Two big, unavoidable reasons: the complexity of language, and the fallibility of gut instinct.

Let's take a closer look at why…

7

LANGUAGE IS SERIOUSLY COMPLICATED; HOW CAN YOU EVER GET IT RIGHT WITHOUT TECH?

WITH SO MANY WORDS, HOW CAN YOU CHOOSE THE RIGHT ONES?

Webster's Third New International Dictionary, Unabridged contains some 470,000 individual entries (if its 1993 Addenda section is counted). This number only takes formal words into consideration, and doesn't account for the slang terms, colloquialisms, emojis, or other linguistic devices that have become a key part of everyday human written communication.

Now add to this the fact that there are also 12 verb tenses in English – the (get ready for it) simple present, simple past, and simple future… the past progressive, present progressive, and future progressive… <takes a breath>… the present perfect, past perfect, and future perfect… and who could forget the present perfect progressive, past perfect progressive, and the future perfect progressive…

You get the point. It's complicated.

And that's just English.

- Spain's *Diccionario de la Real Academia Española* contains approximately 100,000 words.

- Germany's *Der Duden* dictionary contains about 135,000 individual words.

- Russia's *Толко́вый слова́рь живо́го великору́сского языка́* contains 200,000 individual Russian words.

- Italy's *Grande Dizionario Italiano Dell'uso* contains 270,000 individual words.

- China's 汉语大词典 contains 370,000 individual words.

- Japan's 日本国語大辞典 contains 500,000 individual words.

- The 우리말샘, an open online Korean dictionary, contains over 1.1 million individual words, including dialects from both North and South Korean.

Or take French, which has around 100,000 words (again, depending on how you define a 'word'). But – those 100,000 words have about 350,000 different definitions. So, on average, every single word in French has 3.5 different meanings. *C'est la mer à boire*!

If your brand has an international audience, you probably have a headache right now, but the complexity of all of these languages (including English) goes FAR beyond the relatively simple matter of individual word selection. When you think about it, language really is quite fascinating. Or is it captivating? Perhaps it's compelling, engrossing, intriguing, or riveting? Maybe it's more beguiling, or enthralling, or mesmerizing. The choice is yours – and your choice will affect how people respond to your message.

THIS IS YOUR BRAIN… ON WORDS

Language and linguistics are fascinating fields of study, to be sure, as I accidentally found out back in 1997. The human brain has uniquely evolved to deal with it.

Consider this sentence. Or the one above, or the one below. What your brain is doing is fascinating. Your brain is breaking down each sentence into individual words, and then individual characters. You're then building it back up, letter by letter, back into words, and attributing meaning to each of them. Then, you're chunking up word combinations into phrases. At the end of it, you then ascribe meaning to the sentence. You then remember that sentence when you see the next one, and so on, and then derive meaning from the narrative.

Really, it is a fascinating process, but it sure is complicated.

Our ability to understand language is second nature. But, to really understand the complexity of the language – and the arduous cognitive task each of us (and each of your customers) undertakes when reading a sentence – we need to go deeper.

Why does this matter? Because every time you send out a subject line, a call to action or an Instagram caption, your customers' brains are undertaking the process I outlined above. And the words you choose, how you structure them, and how you use them have a huge impact on how your recipient will interpret them.

THE SIX THINGS YOU NEED TO KNOW ABOUT LINGUISTICS

There are six main linguistic elements to consider in your marketing copy. Now, you don't need to memorize these – I haven't – but they're all important and will all affect your copy's performance.

Some make it their life's work to understand linguistics, and there is no shortage of fascinating research into how we as humans communicate. But that's best left for the academics.

Here's what matters for you: it's an undeniable fact that your audience is subconsciously breaking down your copy into its core linguistic components. Luckily for you, the marketing leader, you don't need a PhD in linguistics. But, to fully grasp the complexity of copywriting – and the counterintuitive fact that humans are uniquely bad at it – you need to know the basics.

So bear with me while I briefly outline the six things you need to know about linguistics, specifically pertaining to copywriting.

1 – SYNTAX

Remember learning about the subject and the predicate in grade school? That's syntax: the structure and grammar of language. Syntax does way more than just make a piece of copy readable, though. By playing around with syntax, you can make the boring exciting.

For example, in 2004, the global sportswear giant Adidas built an entire slogan and campaign around rearranging the words 'Nothing is impossible' to read 'Impossible is nothing' to great critical acclaim... and more importantly, a significant jump in sales.

Key take-home: how you structure your marketing language can have a big impact on sales.

2 – PHONETICS

Phonetics[31] – how language sounds – may seem to have very little to do with written marketing language. But, consider this: the human brain doesn't actually interpret the written word. No, instead, as you read this sentence, you're actually reading out loud in your head. In simpler terms: the eyes read, but the brain listens. When you read, your brain translates that to vocal sounds and interprets it – all in your subconscious[32].

If you've ever read a beautiful description of a holiday destination you've never been to and got a picture of it in your mind or imagined the voice when a character in a novel says something, you know what I'm talking about. When your customers read your marketing copy, this same process happens subconsciously. That's why we prefer language that 'rolls off the tongue', whether spoken or written.

Key take-home: if the marketing language you're writing doesn't sound good, it won't read well. And if it doesn't read well, it won't perform well.

3 – MORPHOLOGY

Morphology looks at how words and phrases are formed – things like prefixes, conjugations, and portmanteaus[33]. And this matters! That's why we're shopaholics at supersales, or see romcoms at megaplexes, or have fleeting bromances with our frenemies.

Choosing the right words – and the form of those words – can massively boost how your brand and its marketing are perceived. Ask yourself: would sports megabrand Nike have been as successful if they had told you to 'Just get it done' rather than 'Just do it'? Nope.

Key take-home: choosing your words matters – and choosing the form of your words matters just as much, if not more.

4 – SEMANTICS

Semantics is all about what your message means – and that your message piques your audience's curiosity. The 'sentiment' contained in any piece of text is essentially the meaning that the writer was trying to convey. How that meaning is interpreted by the reader will affect their emotional response to that meaning, and to the text itself.

Semantics is the difference between 'A diamond is forever' and 'A diamond is a very hard, durable stone'.

Key take-home: the sentiment you convey will have a huge impact on results. That's why so much advertising tries to arouse an emotional response.

5 – PUNCTUATION

Let's not forget about the red-headed stepchild of linguistics: punctuation. Formal linguistic theory pays punctuation little mind (if any) since it isn't technically recognized as a part of spoken language. The charlatan's[34]!

That doesn't mean punctuation isn't important, though. The classic example to illustrate the importance of punctuation is, of course, 'Let's eat, Grandma' vs. 'Let's eat Grandma!' The linguistics experts at Phrasee insist that, due to pragmatic factors, the odds of anyone reading 'Let's eat Grandma' and believing that the sender actually wants to eat their grandmother are quite low, but do you really want to take that chance? Your grandma sure doesn't want you to, that's for sure[35].

6 – EMOJI 👍

There's no doubt about it, emoji are cool 😎. They're a new-fangled linguistic construct and can add profound layers of meaning. They also add huge complications to interpretation.

The emoji has proven to function as an extremely effective linguistic shortcut for those communicating cross-culturally, as they visually convey complex concepts in a way that everyone can, in principle, understand. Except for the fact that emojis themselves, for the most part, are devoid of meaning. They exist as contextual amplifiers – so they can make a sarcastic message more sarcastic, or a jubilant message more jubilant, or a sad message even sadder.

They can also cause confusion – ask a grandmother what 🍆 represents and you'll probably get an answer relating to dinner. But ask a millennial, and you'll probably get an answer relating to dessert.

'Language is central to all marketing efforts and has been for decades, with many of the classic slogans still in our minds – "Just Do It", "Diamonds are forever", etc... But today we live in a world overloaded with information and content so it's a huge challenge to create copy that stands out and is memorable. AI-Powered Copywriting has been pivotal in ensuring our brand message not only stands out, but goes further. The technology allows us to truly understand consumer behavior, maximizing its effect and ultimately driving conversion uplift.'

Saul Lopes,
Head of CRM, Dixons Carphone

THE POINT IS: MODERN HUMAN LANGUAGE IS INCREDIBLY COMPLEX

Language is an ever-evolving behemoth of information. Its meanings and interpretations are affected by, on top of linguistic factors, numerous human considerations as well, including context, tone, and intention. It's all quite amazing, if you think about it.

Here's the challenge: it's possible to say almost the exact same thing in millions of different ways. In some cases, even billions. When it comes to writing marketing copy, that matters. For enterprise brands, whose marketing messages reach audiences numbering in the tens of millions, it can matter to the tune of millions of dollars in revenue.

And that ain't no joke[36].

It's nearly impossible for humans to think of all the ways something can be written, due to the plethora of options that exist within language. And yet, to capture The Language Effect, you need to consider all the options, not just a few[37].

Think about it – if there are even just a million ways to convey your message, it would take a human decades to write them all. And if human power alone can't consider all the options, you're massively limiting your probability of success.

This is obviously a big problem. But that's not the only problem you face. Figuring out which phrase is going to work the best is the second, and perhaps more critical, step… and is something humans are uniquely bad at.

“

IT’S POSSIBLE
TO SAY ALMOST
THE EXACT
SAME THING
IN MILLIONS
OF DIFFERENT
WAYS.

”

8

WHY YOU SHOULD NEVER ASK A HUMAN

THE TALE OF LAKE WOBEGON

There's a lovely little town in American folklore that lies in northern Minnesota called Lake Wobegon[38]. It was founded by homesteading German immigrants in the late 19th century. In many ways, Lake Wobegon resembles most other small towns in the American Upper Midwest.

At first glance, you might think there was nothing particularly interesting about this small, picturesque (and, importantly, fictitious) American town. But you'd be wrong. The residents of Lake Wobegon are special. Compared to everyone else in Lake Wobegon:

- all the women who call Lake Wobegon home are exceptionally strong and tall
- all the town's men are exceptionally good-looking and fit
- all its children are of above-average intelligence.

Only a startling 1.3% of Lake Wobegon describe their driving abilities as being below-average when compared to their fellow Lake Wobegonians.

The curious case of Lake Wobegon raises an important question:

How can it be that so many individual members of a population consider themselves to be above-average in so many ways?

The answer is, while their conceit may know no bounds, they simply can't all be above-average. And not only because the town of Lake Wobegon is a work of fiction.

It is simply not possible for the majority of a population to be above-average. That's not how averages work.

1- ILLUSORY SUPERIORITY: WHY PEOPLE AREN'T AS GOOD AS THEY THINK THEY ARE

When left to our own devices to evaluate ourselves and our abilities, we humans have a strong tendency to overestimate our achievements and capabilities. Most of us understand that we're probably not the best at anything. But many of us carry with us the erroneous belief that we are probably above-average at pretty much everything. Hang on a second… how can *most* of us be *above* the average?

Time and time again, humans falsely believe they are superior to others. This fascinating psychological fact has been borne out by study after study and survey after survey across the decades.

While Lake Wobegon itself may be imaginary, the 'Lake Wobegon Effect', as this phenomenon has come to be known, is very real – and is one of the many tricks your mind plays on you.

See, if you think that your team is performing just fine as it is, then you are ignoring the impact you could get by using AI-Powered Copywriting. As philosophically challenging as it may be, you need to accept that human brains are good at many things… but alone they can't generate the most effective copy. The Language Effect requires you to cut through the misinformation your brain is feeding you about how great you already are and focus on a singular goal: better results from your copywriting strategy.

Ask a group of people how good they are at an everyday task – say, cooking, or driving, or writing taglines for online ads. Very few will describe themselves as being below-average at completing that task compared to their peers. This tendency to assume superiority over others lies at the very heart of the Lake Wobegon Effect.

In a 1977 study, 94% of university professors rated themselves as having an above-average IQ in relation to their colleagues. A similar survey was conducted on drivers in the US and Sweden. A substantial majority of respondents – up to 80% – rated themselves as above-average on a number of important driving characteristics[39].

The mathematical truth is that, by definition, most people are average at most things. Outliers certainly exist at the very top and very bottom of the skill spectrum. The vast majority of us, however, fall somewhere in the middle.

According to psychologist Jonathan Shedler PhD, illusory superiority exists as a mechanism to protect our fragile self-esteem from the harsh realities of our own averageness[40]. Wow, harsh! I bet Dr Shedler is very average at parties.

Now, I don't mean to cause offense to those of you thinking that you or your team are above-average at writing copy, but all things being equal, the truth is you're probably very average, and so is your team. And that's OK!

Illusory superiority manifests itself in the minds of copywriters plying their trade for brands across the globe. Most believe that they 'know' the 'best' way to construct a marketing message. Here's the cold, hard truth, though: in most cases, they're wrong.

There are plenty of talented copywriters out there. It's a safe bet that for a small, select group of individuals, it might sometimes be possible to write a perfect line of copy, much like how Mozart could imagine a beautiful sonata. But, aside from this tiny number of outliers, the world is full of Salieris. Remember: Lake Wobegon doesn't exist.

The truth is this: whether or not they have the will or self-awareness to acknowledge it, most copywriters are average copywriters. The copy they write is no better or worse than the copy most of their peers write. This is a statistical fact. But... we all know that average just doesn't cut it in the hyper-competitive digital realm. Only the exceptional stand out, and only those which stand out have a chance of standing the test of time.

2 – COGNITIVE BIASES: WHY YOU CAN'T MAKE A RELIABLY IMPARTIAL CALL (ON ANYTHING)

Cognitive biases are the subconscious prejudices we all have. Like, for example, how I don't enjoy getting punched in the face. Why? Because I have a hardwired belief that getting punched in the face is not enjoyable. My bias toward not getting punched in the face has saved me from getting punched in the face on many occasions. This is a good bias.

But many biases are much more subtle. They're repeated shortcuts in how we deal with the world around us, like how you know to not touch a hot stove, to not hit the gas at a red light, or to avoid accountants at parties. If we didn't have biases to enable us to make decisions in the blink of an eye, humankind would have never evolved. We'd all be in a constant state of paralysis trying to make sense of the world around us. Cognitive biases are what separate us from animals.

These biases permeate every aspect of the human experience, including the small, professional decisions we make every day. Our biases play a huge part in judging the best words and structure to use when writing something as simple as an email subject line. Maybe you have a preference for a certain phrasing that you just can't explain, or maybe a copywriter in your team tells you that something just doesn't look right to them. While on the surface we call this experience and acumen, in reality they are both examples of how cognitive biases can jeopardize your marketing copy.

There are many different types of cognitive bias. Dozens, in fact. For our purposes, we'll focus on a handful. The main biases that inhibit your ability to effectively optimize your brand's marketing language are listed below. How many resonate with you? Be honest.

- **Ambiguity effect:** a tendency to avoid making choices for which the probability of a positive outcome is unclear or unknown.

- **Choice supportive bias:** a tendency to remember one's own decisions as having been better and producing better results than was actually the case.

- **Clustering illusion:** a tendency to lend too much credence to apparent patterns emerging from small runs, short streaks, or small clusters in large samples of random data.
- **Confirmation bias:** a tendency to focus on and interpret information in a way that confirms one's existing preconceptions.
- **Default effect:** a tendency to favor a comfortable default option when presented with several different (and possibly more effective) alternatives.
- **Optimism bias:** a tendency to be overly optimistic and expect favorable outcomes to the choices one makes.
- **Illusion of external agency:** a tendency to view self-generated preferences as the result of, or evidenced by, external sources.

These are just a few of the biases that impact the decisions we make when deciding how to word a piece of marketing copy. We may not be aware of them, but they are always there. They color our interpretations. They determine our preferences. They affect every aspect of every sentence we write.

“

MOST COPYWRITERS ARE AVERAGE COPYWRITERS.

”

BUT: cognitive biases are the #1 enemy of The Language Effect. Here's why.

Picture this: imagine you've tasked your team with writing an email subject line for a sale. Here are just a few of the ways a copywriter's cognitive biases will affect their decision making:

First, a copywriter may eschew an untested or unfamiliar idea of how a message should be constructed (ambiguity effect). She may opt instead for a similar message to one she used on a previous campaign, which she believes worked well (choice supportive bias). Perhaps two or three recent campaigns that went well used a similar structure. She assumes that a similar structure will perform well again (clustering illusion). She thinks she remembers a campaign a few months back that was along these same lines where she used the word 'super sale' which generated a lot of engagement? Yes, she tells herself that did happen (confirmation bias). Then she thinks it's probably best to use 'super sale' again, since it's a safe bet. 'Mega sale' sounds kind of weird she reasons (default effect). Then she convinces herself that this super sale campaign should do just fine (optimism bias). She reassures herself that past performance indicates that 'super sale' is definitely the way to go here (illusion of external agency). Her decision is made, super sale it is.

Is she right? Perhaps 'super sale' will indeed turn out to be the best name for the sale. Maybe the retail brand's subscribers would've agreed that 'mega sale' sounded weird.

BUT: what if the copywriter was wrong?

What if 'mega sale' would've been the best name for the sale in the eyes of the brand's audience? What if the best option was actually 'uber sale', which this individual human had not considered? What if 'uber' generated engagement numbers that put both 'super sale' and 'mega sale' to shame? With cognitive biases at play, neither the copywriter nor the brand would ever know.

That's the real tragedy of cognitive biases in marketing copywriting. Every copywriter has a narrow view of what's good, what's bad, of what will work and what won't. This limits the possibilities for marketing success. There are literally millions of possible ways to structure even a single line of marketing copy. The odds of anyone predicting the best language variant for a given campaign are astronomical to begin with. When cognitive biases is added to the mix… those astronomical odds become insurmountable.

3 – UNCONSCIOUS INCOMPETENCE: WHY YOUR AUTOPILOT NEEDS RESETTING

When a human learns a new task, the brain gets to work. It starts in the part of the brain responsible for figuring out how to perform that task effectively, the hippocampus (which drives our 'working' memory). Once we've mastered the task completely, our hippocampus moves on to figuring out the next problem, and the neocortex (which drives our 'old' memory) takes over. What this basically means is that once we think we've figured out how to do something, we file it in 'Yeah, I already know that' and don't waste any more valuable brain space with it.

You probably experience this phenomenon every time you get behind the wheel of your car. Or every time you ride a bicycle. Or tie your shoe. Or write a subject line. When you've repeated a task so many times – in exactly the same way – you don't even need to think about it anymore. It becomes second nature.

This transition from the hippocampus to the neocortex is entirely involuntary. It's unavoidable and allows us humans to function effectively (most of the time). But what happens if the skill that's been hardwired into your brain wasn't being done effectively in the first place? Or, more worrying still, what happens if external factors change? What if the way you've learned to unconsciously complete a task ceases to be effective?

That's when 'unconscious incompetence' rears its ugly head.

What's unconscious incompetence, you ask? Put simply, it's when you are doing something wrong, and you don't know that you're doing it wrong... a blissfully ignorant incompetence.

Here's an example for you. In the early 2000s, I was working for a media business in London. We put on hundreds of conferences per year, and I had to sign off brochures to go get printed and mailed (yes, postal mail, I'm that old). Anyways, there were so many of them that I got into a routine. I was a lean, mean approval machine. Or so I thought, until the day that my CEO Ruth called me into her office.

Now let me tell you about Ruth. She had come up in a male-dominated industry, and one of her strategies for success was to exude power. Her 80s-esque power suits complemented a fiery mane of red hair. The only thing more fiery than her hair was her ire.

Anyways, Ruth threw a brochure down on the desk, and, using her terse vernacular, abruptly pointed out a glaring typo – a glaring one, I assure you – in the call to action. Erm... WHOOPS!

We were a small team, and I was really busy, so getting into a fast-paced routine was required to get things done on time. Except that... my routine became rote. I had become unconsciously incompetent. And, in my repeated haste, my attention to detail waned, and I signed off and mailed a brochure to about 50,000 people with that mega typo. It still amazes me to this day that I didn't get fired[41].

This kind of unconscious incompetence exists within us all. From the driver who rides the clutch too hard, to the guy in the office who always hits reply-all by accident. We all have our quirks in the ways we complete life's endless minutiae of tasks, and these quirks, by and large involuntary, directly impact how effectively we complete said tasks.

Our autopilot can let us down, particularly for repetitive, relatively simple professional tasks, such as writing an email subject line. It's all too easy to get caught in an ineffective or inefficient cycle. Say you're a copywriter tasked with writing hundreds of subject lines for a travel brand's marketing emails over a period of years. The danger of unconscious incompetence coming into play is very real. It can have a significant impact on your email marketing's performance.

Here's an example. US craft giant JOANN send millions of emails throughout the year. As with many retailers, their bread and butter email campaigns are their general promotion emails. For years, they followed the status quo and these subject lines would prominently feature the discount that was being offered. So, when JOANN started using Phrasee, the results astounded them. Phrasee's AI, of course, doesn't have a hippocampus or a neocortex, so cognitive biases and unconscious incompetence don't come into play.

Anyways, the JOANN team tested their own language – X% off a product – versus what Phrasee's AI generated… which didn't mention the discount whatsoever. And guess what? The non-discounted language won by a country mile.

It's not that the JOANN team was incompetent. Nothing could be further from the truth! But after writing hundreds of subject lines over the years, their collective neocortex took over.

You've probably experienced this yourself! When an email's deadline is fast approaching and your team needs to come up with a subject line for it ASAP… chances are, your team's hippocampus takes a back seat. That is to say, your team is on autopilot. The good news is: they're not alone!

'I think as marketers we get into a room, and sometimes we overthink it, like "hey we gotta tell them that this product is on sale." But from a customer standpoint, we really started to understand, don't focus on the offer as much, but focus on the engagement.'

Lee Washington II,
CRM & Loyalty Strategy Manager, JOANN Stores

Picture this: imagine a copywriter writing subject lines at a time when using lots of CAPS was generating increased engagement. Plus, perhaps she also saw great results from sticking emojis in there too. Early positive reinforcement in the form of high open rates or ROI numbers rolled in. Habits were formed. The neocortex's autopilot took charge. Using capitalization and emojis in email subject line copy simply became second nature to her.

Now imagine it's one year later. Now too many CAPS are spam red-flags. And all the competitors are using emojis in their subject lines too, so they are no longer visual differentiators. Performance numbers began to dip. When asked to explain this, the copywriter could only draw a blank. She was doing what she'd always done. She was an expert at this, after all!

To see past one's own unconscious incompetence is a Herculean task. It's often only when presented with irrefutable evidence to the contrary that we become capable of seeing how our own beliefs have been holding us back… and ultimately limiting our success.

You're not alone in this most human condition. In fact, you're in good company – every single human being on the planet has the exact same problem.

Finding the optimal copy with which to broadcast your brand's message to the world is a very complex problem. Too complex a problem to leave entirely to the instincts of fallible human copywriters, especially when that message is destined to appear side by side with similar messages from your competitors.

ADD IT ALL UP, AND COPYWRITING IS WAY HARDER THAN YOU THOUGHT

Every time you send an email, or serve a Facebook ad, or update your website, or whatever you're doing, there's language – and your customers will be reading it. Your customers will be subconsciously deconstructing the language into the linguistic components, like semantics and pragmatics, and will ascribe meaning to it. They'll then pass it through their cognitive bias filters, and then decide whether or not to take action.

This is exactly the unconscious cognitive process you followed when I showed you those 10 Virgin Holidays subject lines a few pages back.

Here's exactly what your brain did, albeit unconsciously:

1. You read the lines, and, in the blink of an eye, you deconstructed them into individual linguistic components, like words and phrases.

2. You then read them to yourself in your brain's voice, and as you read it, ascribed meaning, context, and sentiment to them.

3. You then passed all of this information through your cognitive biases, and, in a hidden Excel table in your mind, gave each an implied performance score.

4. Lastly, you ranked all the performance scores and determined that one subject line was the best one.

All that happened in a split second. Humans are amazing!

And yet – chances are you got it wrong. But that's OK, because most people would have gotten it wrong too! This is a very taxing cognitive process to follow, one that is permeated by pitfalls. These pitfalls, simply put, are unconsciously driving you to pick ineffective language.

And these pitfalls are probably costing you millions of dollars.

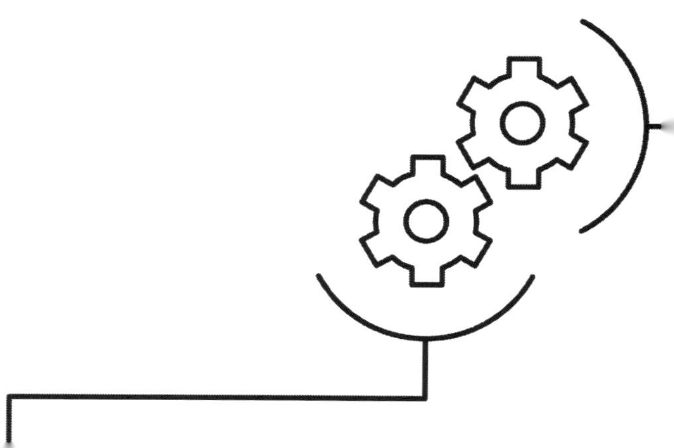

PART 3

GETTING STARTED WITH AI-POWERED COPYWRITING

'If there's a new way, I'll be the first in line

But it better work this time'

Peace Sells... But Who's Buying?
Megadeth

9

A TALE OF TWO STRATEGIES

GET READY TO BE A GAME CHANGER

I hope that your eyes are now opened to the huge opportunity The Language Effect and its enabler, AI-Powered Copywriting, offer you. But – it's not as simple as just saying, 'Let's do this,' and waiting for a magic unicorn to poop cash money all over your desk. You need to decide how you're going to go about it, and you have two options.

LONG TERM VS. SHORT TERM

The first thing you'll need to figure out is exactly what 'optimized' copy looks like for your brand. There are two distinct strategies to choose from, each with its own benefits and drawbacks.

Here's how they work:

LONG-TERM: FOCUS ON THE LONG TERM (SIX MONTHS+) RESULTS

This strategy focuses on evaluating the long-term effects of copy across the lifespan of your marketing program, continually honing and changing the language you use on each channel based on results.

Strategic goals:

- Build sustainable audience relationships by focusing on your brand's voice and improving it over time.
- Maximize the performance of a given marketing channel over time with an eye toward long-term performance.
- Learn what types of copy resonate with your brand's audience – not just focusing on today, but also on tomorrow, next week, next month and next year.

Benefits:

- Delivery of fresh content for every campaign.
- Development and maintenance of a strong, unique brand voice.
- Drives long-term engagement, audience trust, and increased revenue over time.

Drawbacks:

- Doesn't necessarily generate the highest possible performance uplift for each individual campaign.

Method:

This is the strategy that underpins The Language Effect. It requires high technology, an open mind, and a strong belief in your brand. The results won't shock-and-awe – they're not designed to – but they will deliver, week in and week out.

SHORT-TERM: FOCUS ON SHORT-TERM (JUST YOUR NEXT CAMPAIGN) RESULTS

Strategic goal:

- Maximize the performance of a single campaign.
- Continue attempting to maximize the performance of every subsequent campaign individually.

Benefits:

- Possibility of higher revenue in the short term.
- Possibility of immediate uplift in an individual campaign's performance.

Drawbacks:

- Lack of consideration of brand voice or consumer brand perception.
- Potential for damage to brand-to-customer relationships.
- Early response spikes that are not sustainable over time (we call this 'performance decay').
- High occurrence of unsubscribes due to spammy brute force tactics, such as deceptive, pushy, misleading, and over-promising language.
- Loss of long-run revenue and brand trust.

Method:

For this strategy to work, you need copy that shocks-and-awes people into engaging with your marketing. This is pretty easy – all you need is a database of pre-tested phrases – phrases that have been used in another brand's marketing. Many of these phrases, however, will have adverse long-term effects on consumer perceptions of your brand

and its marketing. **It's this strategy that led us down the clickbait race to the bottom. And trust me – that's a race you don't want to win.**

THE DANGERS OF SHORT-TERMISM

Obviously, short-term results are important. I'm not going to pretend that they aren't. The quest for KPI uplift and quick wins has been driving change and innovation in the marketing game for decades.

DANGER NO. 1: YOUR CUSTOMERS STOP TRUSTING YOU

Incentivizing 'quick wins' has created an inefficient marketing landscape. Simply put, your short-termism is probably running roughshod over the brand equity and trust you have spent countless marketing dollars building over the years.

If a short-term uptick in marketing performance is your primary goal, there is no shortage of tricks available that a marketer can make use of to deliver it – consider deceptive email subject lines that begin with phrases like 'Regarding your order', 'Urgent', or 'Action required'... or the egregious false 'RE:'s and 'FW:'s. Once a consumer clicks through to your website, they realize they've been baited-and-switched and are left feeling bitter toward your brand. Each of these sketchy methods is 100% guaranteed to increase the likelihood that your audience will engage with your marketing… once. Maybe twice if you're lucky. And then your audience will switch off because they'll no longer trust you.

DANGER NO. 2: YOU FORGET ABOUT TOMORROW

But – and it's an important but – marketing is not purely a quantitative endeavor. By purely focusing on what's happening today, we become short-sighted. When we purely consider today's spreadsheet, we get gains today – but forego gains tomorrow.

Spreadsheet-driven marketing is the scourge of the modern marketer. It forces you to make short-term decisions, and it soon becomes an institutional norm. 'Forget brand voice – we need more opens and clicks… NOW!' says the devil on your shoulder. But the devil can't see beyond today and doesn't care about tomorrow.

The marketer of the future must learn to silence the devil… and listen to the angel.

The question is: are the relationships you've built with your audience and the unique voice you've established for your brand worth sacrificing for a few extra engagements, click-throughs, or opens in the short term?

While the devil may suggest yes… the angel's answer is definitely no.

SPREADSHEET-DRIVEN MARKETING IS THE SCOURGE OF THE MODERN MARKETER.

DANGER NO. 3: YOUR BRAND'S AUTHENTIC VOICE GETS LOST AND FORGOTTEN

Take a look at these six email subject lines from six household name brands, all sent within a recent two-week period. (We've redacted the brand names to avoid embarrassing them.)

RETAILER 1	RETAILER 2
:-) [REDACTED] You've been granted this >>	(1) friendly message You've been granted NEW SURPRISE POINTS!

RETAILER 3	RETAILER 4
Secret alert! You've been granted a BONUS	Please read: You've been granted Free Air

RETAILER 5	RETAILER 4
Secret alert! You've been granted 4 free issues	CONGRATS! You've been granted access to our Flash Sale

These subject lines appeared in the inboxes of millions of consumers around the world. And, whether the emails themselves were opened or not, they all made an impression.

Ask yourself: is using the exact same copy as at least five other brands the best way to create a memorable brand impression for your audience?

It's a safe bet that there's a performance-based reason all these brands made use of the phrase 'you've been granted' in this instance. Presumably, this phrase performed well in one brand's send(s), so whoever provided these subject lines decided to use it for everyone. Viewed from the short-term perspective, this is quite a logical approach.

Viewed from the long-term perspective, however, the benefits of such tactics are far outweighed by the potential damage to the brand and its customer relationships.

How many times can individual consumers see the words 'you've been granted' in their inbox before those words begin to look like just another spammy marketing message? Using this phrase over and over again will show decreasing returns over time – and that's a fact. At Phrasee, we call this phenomenon 'performance decay'. Any phrase, no matter how effective, invariably becomes less effective over time... and even more so when everyone is saying the same thing!

The negatives associated with short-termism in marketing copy run far deeper than just a tendency toward repetitive language, however.

DANGER NO. 4: YOU'RE STUCK IN A CLICKBAIT RACE TO THE BOTTOM

It's a similar story for brands that make use of 'race to the bottom' discounting in their marketing. A 50% or 70% discount offer is sure to raise a few eyebrows and drive engagement. This is particularly true for brands that have managed to build a high level of perceived value through effective branding and marketing in the past.

An ad reading '50% off Ferraris all month long!' would likely be Ferrari's highest performing ad campaign of all time. Knowing this, one could make the case that '50% off Ferraris all month long!' represents the pinnacle of marketing copy optimization for the Ferrari brand. But, for numerous reasons, the short-term gains Ferrari would experience probably wouldn't be worthwhile. Sure, Ferrari would sell a lot of cars this month, but for how long could the brand absorb such hefty cuts to its profit margins? Further, how many '50% off' campaigns could Ferrari run before no one would be willing to pay full price for a Ferrari ever again?

This Ferrari nightmare is an extreme example, and the brand is highly unlikely to ever offer a 50% discount (or a discount of any kind, for that matter). But here in the real world, a similar scenario has been playing out in the retail sector, with some brands eschewing a sustainable long-term strategy in exchange for short-term gains, often to their own detriment. Other brands, meanwhile, have kept their eyes firmly focused on the long-term horizon.

Let's take a look at an example which is much more firmly rooted in reality: the divergent paths of two of the world's largest retailers (again anonymized to avoid embarrassment). Let's call them 'Retailer A' and 'Retailer B'...

Retailer A was a well-established retail brand with stores in almost every North American city back in 2000. But the brand had fallen on hard times. Falling revenues, stiff competition from brands like Amazon and Walmart, and an aging customer-base had driven the retailer close to bankruptcy. Store closures abounded, costing billions of shareholder value, and putting thousands of jobs at risk.

With the pressure on, Retailer A needed immediate sales to stay afloat. The brand simply didn't have the luxury of a long-term marketing approach. As a result, the brand opted for discount offers on a grand scale and a marketing strategy built on short-term revenue gains at all costs. Retailer A's sales revenues increased for a short time, allowing the company to avoid bankruptcy and many of the additional job losses that its employees feared.

But, as the deep-discounting race to the bottom eroded Retailer A's profit margins, the marketing copy proclaiming yet another 'big sale' gradually became white noise to the discerning ears of consumers. Just take a look at the below graph comparing the two retailers' stock prices over the same period of time (January 2016 – December 2019).

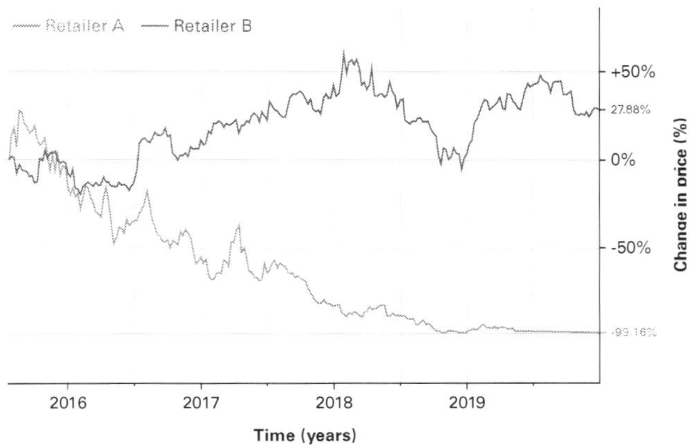

Comparing the stock price of Retailer A and Retailer B (January 2016 – December 2019[42])

Over the ensuing years, Retailer A's stock price plummeted. Meanwhile, in another corner of the retail sector, Retailer B was in a different sort of trouble. It had been making use of short-term tactics in its marketing for years. Its digital marketing efforts – rife with discount language and clever ploys to capture consumer attention – had begun to sputter.

The brand's digital marketing engagement rates were decaying. And that was very bad news. On top of that, Retailer B's margins were taking a serious hit at the hands of the ever-increasing discounts the company was offering in an effort to buoy its flagging engagement numbers.

Retailer B made the tough decision to change direction with its digital marketing efforts. The company abandoned the short-term tactics which it had been leaning on, opting instead to focus on building its brand through a sustained long-term strategy.

Since deciding to embrace a long-term marketing vision, driven by a long-term marketing copy approach, Retailer B (obviously, by sheer coincidence, a Phrasee customer) has seen its stock price more than double.

Should the contrasting overall performance of Retailer A and Retailer B be attributed purely to the marketing copy choices the two brands made? Certainly not. There are myriad factors at play in the worlds of retail and marketing in the digital age. But The Language Effect – and its enabler, AI-Powered Copywriting – had a real impact on the divergent outcomes of two huge brands.

LET'S TAKE A CLOSER LOOK AT LONG-TERM AND SHORT-TERM LANGUAGE

The copy you use is a crucial factor in implementing any overall branding or marketing strategy. This makes your decision between long-term and short-term an extremely important one.

The decision you make here, and how that decision manifests in your brand's marketing copy both now and in the future, will be a significant factor in the long-term outlook of your brand.

For Retailer A and Retailer B, the choice between long-term and short-term is apparent in many aspects of each brand's marketing over the past few years. Nowhere is this more apparent than in the email subject line copy each brand uses to engage its audience.

SHORT-TERM LANGUAGE AS USED BY RETAILER A	LONG-TERM LANGUAGE AS USED BY RETAILER B
(1) new message. you've been granted THESE savings	Check out these Tuesday savings (whoa!)
Valued Customer, PLEASE DON'T IGNORE these savings	You've never seen savings like these before!
IMPORTANT NOTICE: You deserve some deals	👋 Hey there … you're so close to a great discovery
This is MEGA-URGENT, Valued Customer! Please don't overlook these deals	Ready, set, save!
Savings enclosed. PLEASE OPEN ASAP!	If you love deals, check these out
Your deals are confirmed ✅ omgomgomgomg…	We keep the DEALS coming

Short-termism has clear benefits – if all you care about is this quarter's target and not the future, then it's the strategy for you.

However, there are very few brands for which this is the case. Perhaps Retailer A, as they needed immediate sales to stay afloat and didn't have the luxury of considering the future. Perhaps consistently using brute-force-discounts over and over and over to drive short-term sales was a sound strategic approach for Retailer A at the time. But ask yourself this: why would you EVER pay full price for an item at Retailer A? You wouldn't… and their customers didn't.

Consider the inverse – a brand that chooses to focus on positioning their brand for long-term success, like Retailer B did, instead of taking the easier route of using short-term tactics to drive short-term sales.

Since Retailer B moved on to a long-term strategy in its marketing (shameless plug: with a little help from Phrasee!), they've been consistently able to increase email audience engagement performance compared to non-optimized, human-written email subject line copy. It works out to an uplift of over 11% more consumers seeing their offerings – a consistent 11% increase across three years.

We may not have access to similar data on Retailer A's email marketing performance. Still, if the company's stock price is any indication, we think it's safe to say that short-termism has fallen far short of the long-term revenue-driving needs of a struggling brand in a shifting retail landscape.

BUT THE SHORT-TERMIST TREND IS SHIFTING

The brands like Retailer A, who fail to recognize and adapt to this new reality and still rely upon short-term clickbait tactics are being left behind by those who do.

It's not just me espousing this viewpoint. No, I'm not alone, not by a long shot. Take Adidas' global media director Simon Peel, who recently told *Marketing Week*[43] magazine: 'Short-termism is always going to exist. But what we're trying to do is to make sure that while we're doing that, we also look after the long-term health of the brand and know that behind those short-term deliveries, the brand is the one that ultimately delivers against them.'

Or, the head of experience at WPP agency Wavemaker, Noah Mallin[44]: 'There's a mindset of, "Tell me what's happening this quarter, don't get me involved in three quarters from now" ... but there are a lot of brands that are realizing that there's a point at which all of the direct-response marketing and all of the price messaging just stops being effective, or effective as it was. For people that get hooked on it, you do it and do it, you end up needing more and more to get to the same place more and more. Once consumers become acclimated to the idea that you're willing to discount and that's a huge part of the messaging, they won't buy until they see that message again.'

Or perhaps the most succinct example yet, the CFO of Gap Inc, Teri List-Stoll[44], who said that they have 'frankly become too heavily dependent on messaging around discounting as opposed to bigger-picture brand messaging, focusing on product and value that we know resonates with the Old Navy consumer.'

WHAT IF YOU DIDN'T HAVE TO CHOOSE?

The never-ending quest for consumer engagement is currently driving the world's brands headlong toward a new marketing paradigm. In this new paradigm, it's not just *how much* engagement your marketing delivers that matters. *How* your brand achieves that engagement has become just as important.

The brands like Retailer A, who fail to recognize and adapt to this new reality and still rely upon short-term clickbait tactics, are being left behind by those who do.

The choice between 1) optimizing marketing copy to deliver a consistent brand voice and a positive audience experience in the long term; or 2) optimizing marketing copy to deliver better performance and more revenue in the short term, has proven to be a tough one indeed for many brands and marketers.

But what if there were a way to optimize your marketing language to deliver a consistent brand voice, a positive audience experience, and a better revenue-driving performance, all at the same time?

What if I told you that choosing one strategy doesn't mean foregoing the other completely? It's not a black-and-white scenario, so it's not a binary decision.

What we are really looking at is better described as a spectrum.

Deciding where your brand's marketing should fall within this spectrum is the key to maximizing the performance-enhancing effects of better marketing copy – the very essence of The Language Effect.

Maximizing your response rates WITHOUT sacrificing the long-term viability of your brand is exactly what The Language Effect is all about.

Indeed, there is a way to have your cake and eat it too… and now, I'll tell you how.

10

BRAND VOICE OR RESULTS: HOW ABOUT BOTH?

YOUR BRAND VOICE HAS TO BE AUTHENTIC

In 1999, the American cyclist Lance Armstrong was on top of the world. After overcoming the metastatic testicular cancer that had forced him out of cycling in 1996, Armstrong staged an amazing comeback and won the 1999 Tour de France – cycling's premier global event – by a healthy margin. He became, for all intents and purposes, an American hero.

Armstrong's tale of overcoming tragedy and adversity and raising $500 million for his charity to support people affected by cancer around the world inspired many.

Over the next several years, Lance Armstrong was awarded almost every title and accolade the world of cycling had to offer. Through pure American grit and determination, the legend went, Armstrong had overcome one of life's most terrifying obstacles and come out of it even better than ever.

What. A. Dude.

To put it plainly, Lance Armstrong was one hell of a brand. The sponsorship dollars rained down. Armstrong became one of the most celebrated and financially successful athletes America has ever produced (and that's a long list!). Everybody wanted to hitch their wagon to the Lance Armstrong train.

Why?

Lance Armstrong's name, and what he represented, were the perfect marketing message. Not only was he performing at a pretty much unparalleled level in his sport, his brand voice – that of a cancer-surviving super-athlete – was above reproach.

Or so it seemed…

In his successful quest to attain optimal cycling performance, Lance Armstrong engaged in some questionable tactics.

To be blunt, Lance Armstrong used performance-enhancing drugs. He used them a lot. He told Oprah so in a revealing and heartbreaking interview in 2013, and everyone saw it. For a brand like Lance Armstrong, for which the medium literally was the message, this was very bad news indeed. An overzealous desire to maximize performance destroyed Lance Armstrong's once-mighty brand voice.

Neither Lance Armstrong nor the Lance Armstrong brand has ever recovered from his much-publicized doping scandal. Chances are, neither ever will.

The saddest part of this very sad tale is that it didn't have to be this way.

He could have been an American hero without cheating. Pity no-one told him so…

The short-term 'strategy' (if we can call it that) we laid out in the previous chapter is like steroids for marketing. Sure, you'll get a short-term boost in performance off the back of dishonest tactics, but eventually, your audience will realize that you've been cheating and turn their backs on you. As Lance Armstrong can attest, once you've been branded a cheater (or a spammer) it can be a very tough label to overcome.

The question is: what would've happened if Lance Armstrong had focused his considerable talents and energies on a long-term approach instead?

Let's say Lance Armstrong could've beaten cancer and staged an incredible comeback – without the use of steroids – that saw him become the second-best cyclist in the world. Or the fourth-best. Even the tenth-best. How much less marketable would he and his brand have been, really?

Instead of focusing on being the underdog that came back to be a world-class athlete (a laudable and highly marketable story in itself), he instead wanted to be invincible. His quest to be a Superman amongst Average Joes led him to focus on short-termism and winning at all costs.

As it turns out, short-termism was his kryptonite.

DON'T (EVER) LOSE YOUR BRAND VOICE FOR THE SAKE OF A QUICK WIN

> **'Email marketing is a key marketing channel for Domino's Pizza. But, in today's overcrowded inboxes, our challenge was to stay relevant, increase KPIs, and not spam people. Phrasee's AI honed in on what makes our audience tick... and our email results have been awesome ever since.'**
>
> ***Nicola Keane, CRM Manager, Domino's Pizza***

Nobody wants to forego optimal performance. This is just as true in marketing as it is in cycling. But it's crucial to remember that sustainable success can only be found in striking the right balance between performance and brand.

Marketing performance matrix

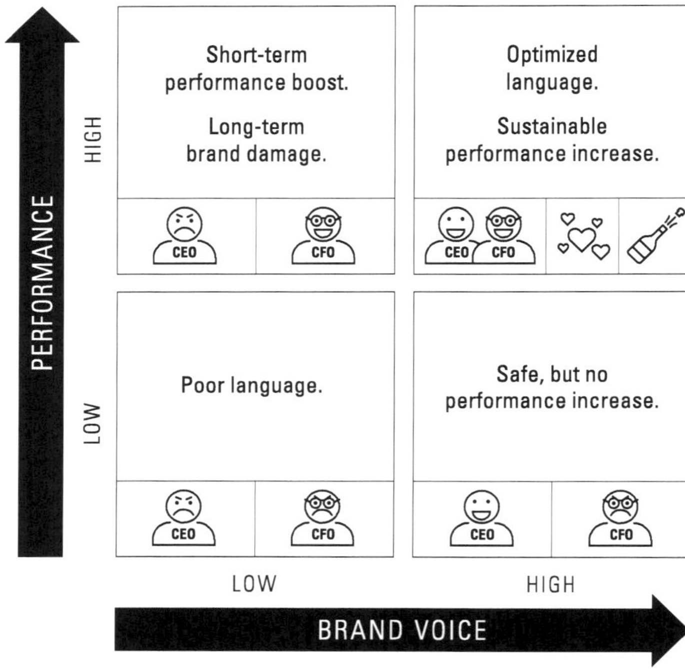

Key

Better marketing performance through optimized copy is great, that's for sure... with one, huge caveat: optimized copy must be in your brand's voice.

See the matrix on the left. The vertical axis represents marketing copy performance as measured by the stated goal you want that copy to achieve. The horizontal axis represents the copy's adherence to your brand's unique tone of voice.

Marketing copy that neither performs well nor adheres to your brand voice is just plain useless. Don't do that, for neither your CEO nor your CFO will be happy. Such language falls into the bottom left-hand corner of the matrix.

Marketing copy that adheres strictly to your brand's voice but doesn't perform well isn't much good either because, well... it doesn't perform. Your CEO loves it, but your CFO hates it. So don't do that, either. This copy falls into the bottom right-hand corner of the matrix.

Marketing copy that performs well but doesn't adhere to your brand voice might seem tempting on its surface, but don't be fooled. Such copy may give your marketing performance a short-term boost but will cost your relationship with your audience in the long run. Your CFO will pat you on the back, but your CEO will kick you in the ass. This is found in the top-left quadrant.

Peak marketing copy performance is found in the top right-hand corner of the matrix above, where optimal marketing performance intersects with optimal brand voice. This, at the top right of the matrix, is the perfect scenario. Both your CEO and CFO are happy. You smash your targets. Your customers love you. You are soon crowned the all-encompassing Monarch of Marketing. A statue of your likeness is erected in your boardroom (OK, maybe I'm over-exaggerating, but dare to dream!).

This is The Language Effect – high performing copy that builds your brand. So how can you achieve this marketing Valhalla? Let me introduce you to AI-Powered Copywriting.

11

WHY AI IS THE FUTURE OF COPYWRITING... AND THE FUTURE IS NOW

INVENTION IS 2% INSPIRATION AND 98% PERSPIRATION

If you indulge me for a moment, I'd like to tell a story about my father. His name is Howard Malm and he is a very clever man. He's a physicist, an inventor, an engineer, and has a PhD. But, above all, he's a creative problem solver. I like to think that I take after him in this sense (also: baldness from the age of 28. Thanks a lot, Dad!).

In my quest to solve The Language Effect, I took inspiration from one particular engineering problem that my father solved for the oil and gas industry back in the early 2000s.

My dad was trying to improve the fuel efficiency of huge natural gas engines. These massive units are owned and operated by oil and gas production companies such as BP, Esso, and Shell. Since fuel is a mega cost for such companies, reducing fuel usage through this stage of the production process represented an enormous cost decrease. Plus, the inefficiencies in these processes were leaking large amounts of natural gas into the atmosphere, so improved technology also meant an impressive reduction in greenhouse gas emissions. Win-win!

The available solutions at the time were expensive and rarely installed. But, since these oil/gas companies were leaking fuel and money every day, Dad wanted to implement a cost-effective solution he'd invented[45].

However, even after verifying the viability in a temporary field trial, he was unable to convince others in his company that his unconventional solution was a worthwhile investment.

The company my father worked for at the time was not willing to propose his solution to the engine owners and operators. It was only after he calculated that his solution could save an operator 10% to 30% of their annual fuel costs that anyone finally listened. The reduction in emissions also led to further savings, as various governments had begun to legislate policy to monetarily incentivize carbon reduction.

Once the new equipment was installed and running at an engine-compressor site, it worked (in my dad's words) 'like a hot-damn!' According to the amount of waste gas previously vented at each site, the fuel savings could vary between 2% to over 30% of a company's annual fuel costs; that's $10,000 to $150,000 per year, per unit.

Put simply, my father was right, and he proved it[46]. He overcame many obstacles on his journey toward implementing his advanced technological solution to a real-world problem. To date, his concept has saved oil and gas companies massive amounts of money and, more importantly, untold damage to our planet's atmosphere.

He even took some of his profits and founded a scholarship at his alma mater for research into countering climate change with science[47].

What. A. Dude.

My father believes that it is 'absolutely true that invention is 2% inspiration and 98% perspiration'. This message was imprinted on me from an early age, and it has been a driving force behind my ongoing effort to make Phrasee the most effective AI-Powered Copywriting solution on the planet.

Some problems are simple, and some are complex. This fact is true in life, it's true in business, and it's true in marketing. As we've already seen, the problem of optimizing marketing language to deliver better digital marketing outcomes falls into the 'complex' category. Maybe not quite as complex as figuring out how to reduce waste gas at an oil and gas plant, but complex in its own way, nonetheless.

SO, HOW CAN WE MAXIMIZE THE LANGUAGE EFFECT?

There are three options currently available for optimizing your brand's marketing language to bring your brand more sales:

1. Let your copywriters do their thing (remember they are fallible humans) and hope that the knowledge they gain helps them do it better... and pray they don't quit.
2. Identify some keywords and phrases that have worked for your brand (and others) in the past and use them in your marketing language, and pray these words don't suffer performance deterioration, and that no one else uses them.
3. Use AI-powered technology to optimize your brand's marketing language at scale.

We've discussed the first two options on this list in previous chapters of this very book. But, just to be clear, let's recap on why these strategies might be less than ideal for your brand.

1. If you continue letting your copywriters write your brand's marketing copy based on their own intuition and gut feel about what will work, you'll continue seeing similar results to what you've seen in the past. Remember the old saying: 'if you do what you've always done, you're gonna get what you always got.' Your copywriters will keep on writing their same marketing copy. Sometimes it'll be effective, and sometimes it won't. As digital marketing channels and audiences continue to grow and change, the scale of language your brand needs will increase. You'll have to hire more (and more) copywriters to meet the growing need for copy. If you're lucky, you'll hire good ones. If you aren't, you'll hire bad ones, but you'll probably hire average ones and the effectiveness of your marketing language will decline over time.

2. If you choose the second option and adopt a strategy which retrofits words and phrases that have worked for your brand or someone else's in the past, you may see a short-term uplift in marketing language performance, which is great! However, over time your brand voice will suffer because your marketing will begin to sound just like everyone else's. Your

relationship with your audience will suffer, reducing your overall marketing engagement, which isn't so great.

3. Which brings us to option three. If you forego the first two options (and their obvious drawbacks) and opt instead to seek out an advanced, data-based technological solution (like my dear old dad did!), you really only have one practical, effective option: artificial intelligence.

But wait… what's that I hear you say? 'There's NO WAY a machine could write like a human, and NO FRIGGIN' WAY a machine could write BETTER than a human!'

There is a way. An incredible way. A way that's making brands around the world millions of dollars every day. A way that will capture The Language Effect today, tomorrow, and the day after.

12

HOW PHRASEE'S AI-POWERED COPYWRITING WORKS

THE STRUGGLE IS REAL

Hello, and welcome to the shameless plug zone.

Well, sort of. This book is a labor of love, a passion of mine from start to finish. The psychological, economic, and technical underpinnings of AI-Powered Copywriting are the culmination of my life's work.

So, I hope it's been an interesting read thus far.

But I'd be remiss if I didn't talk about the tech we've built that solves the very problem we're all facing.

So, well, perhaps this is a bit of a sales pitch. But this isn't something I'm apologizing for. The problem is real, and one you probably face right now. The solution is real too, I know, because I've spent years making it happen.

The problem is this: when it comes to the copy we choose to use to speak to our audience, we just can't be confident what's best. Sure, we can split test a few options, but I'm talking about taking all the words and all the combinations of those words possible and choosing the best one for our specific audience. We're blind. We'd be better off going to Vegas and putting it all on black thirteen[48].

Not only that but we, as marketers, have hitherto been rendered powerless by the whims of not just our gut instincts, but everyone else's too. We would never dream of telling an engineer how to build a bridge or telling a ballerina how to improve their point. And yet, everyone and their dog gives their opinions on copywriting. Why? Because we never had cold, hard data to back up our copywriting. We were powerless, and it sucked.

So, what is the solution to powerlessness?
Simple: POWER.

That's why I started Phrasee – to empower brands and marketers with AI-Powered Copywriting. To save brands from the vagaries of their teams' gut feelings. To help brands capture The Language Effect – and to use it to their advantage.

WHAT DOES PHRASEE DO?

> **'We suspected that Phrasee's AI-optimized marketing copy would have a positive impact on our audience engagement, but we had no idea how big that impact would actually be... the results we've seen from giving Phrasee a try have been nothing short of amazing!'**
>
> ***Ian McKenna, CRM Analyst, Superdry***

Anyways, you're probably wondering what, exactly, Phrasee does.

What Phrasee does is awesome enough for Gartner to name Phrasee a Cool Vendor in 2018 (how cool that makes me at parties, however, is questionable). CB Insights, the analyst firm, named us 2017's Most Innovative AI Company. Wow! And in 2016, I was named Tech Entrepreneur of the Year at the UK Business Awards[49], alongside Phrasee winning the Best New Business trophy.

What Phrasee does is awesome enough for some of the world's leading brands to use our tech on a daily basis. In fact, I bet that you've already bought something as a direct result of language that Phrasee has generated.

What Phrasee does is awesome enough to be used in nearly every possible form of advertising – from email marketing, to push messages, to SMS, to social ads, and all points in between.

What Phrasee does is cool. And here's how it works.

1. You brief Phrasee like you would brief a copywriter. In fact, it's even easier – because Phrasee doesn't talk back!

2. You then click the Magic Button (and yes, we have a magic button in the platform, because of course we do!).

3. Phrasee generates thousands upon thousands of human-sounding variants of marketing copy, all in your brand's voice. How? We have built a sophisticated **Natural Language Generation (NLG)** system. It's basically a programming language to generate language. Our team of computational linguists code a language model bespoke to each customer's brand. It's pretty amazing, and I'm not just saying that because I'm incredibly biased.

4. Once we have thousands of versions, we input them into our **Deep Learning Engine** and the output is a ranked order of predicted performance. The system doesn't look at human-defined variables like length or

emotion. Why? Because these are constructs the human brain has created but are not the constructs that humans actually respond to. The human brain is much more complex, and so is our system. Our neural net looks at thousands of parameters and spots infinitesimal patterns that are hidden to the human eye. It doesn't suffer from human problems of cognitive bias – instead, it lets the data do the talking.

5. The end result when you combine our NLG and deep learning systems? You get high-performing copy to use in your campaigns… all at the click of a button.

6. Oh yeah – all of that happens in real-time and takes under 10 seconds. There are no humans involved, so there's no delay.

7. And that's not all! Using a method called **transfer learning**, we can take the learnings from one language model, say, for example, email subject lines, and extrapolate it across other channels, for example, Facebook ads, Google ads, push messages or web copy. What that means is that you use your email marketing as a petri dish. And once the scientists make a discovery, spread the results across all of your marketing.

You maximize The Language Effect across all your marketing channels and make bank. Boom.

'After seeing what Phrasee did for our email marketing campaigns, we expected it to deliver on our social campaigns as well. What we didn't expect was a MASSIVE 31% decrease in our cost per lead (CPL)! Delivering increased efficiency like that is very impressive and we're excited to continue testing Phrasee across our social media campaigns.'

Alexis Harrison,
Head of External Media, Wowcher

Now, of course, there's a lot more going on behind the scenes. A huge amount more. Over the last five years, we've built, tweaked, rebuilt, retweaked and optimized the system. Hundreds of customer calls led to hundreds of updates. Thousands of user sessions led to thousands of tweaks. And millions of words and phrases, written by Phrasee's AI in real-time, led to untold millions in extra revenue for our customers.

What matters most is this: our NLG system has been honed over the last five years to become a world-leading (and unique) piece of technology, unlike anything else on the planet[50]. Our deep learning engine can predict the performance of copy better than any human anywhere on the planet Earth.

There really is nothing else like it in the world – Phrasee is a truly unique snowflake in a blizzard of homogenous technology.

Phrasee is the only technology on the planet that empowers you to benefit from The Language Effect. Phrasee lets you maximize the impact of your marketing copy without compromising your brand voice. Phrasee is changing the world, one phrase at a time.

Sure, I'm biased when I say Phrasee is awesome. But just because I'm biased doesn't mean I'm wrong.

PART 4

THE FUTURE OF MARKETING

'We're the future

Your future'

God Save the Queen
Sex Pistols

13

THE HISTORY AND FUTURE OF AI-POWERED COPYWRITING

LIFE BEFORE SPREADSHEET SOFTWARE

Accounting was once laborious, monotonous, complicated work. It involved reams of notebooks called 'ledgers'. Each ledger was made up of sheets of blank cells, each sheet of blank cells spread across from one side of the ledger's fold to the other – hence the name 'spreadsheet'.

Each entry on a spreadsheet cell needed to be manually written in with a pencil. Since the data in each cell in a spreadsheet's chain of cells often altered the data in all subsequent cells in the chain, a change in one cell's data typically meant changes in dozens of other cells were required, and had to be made manually by armies of accountants with erasers, pencils, and calculators in hand. Imagine a world without spreadsheets... everything would seem impossible. No wonder they had to fake the moon landing[51]!

A company's accounting system often involved the use of dozens of separate ledgers and spreadsheets, the data from which was compiled into a larger 'master' spreadsheet. This master spreadsheet contained the data upon which a company's most important decisions were based. As such, it was essential that every calculation contained within was accurate and free from error.

Then, you had layers of checkers to make sure no one had messed up. Luckily for most companies, accountants were generally exceedingly well-trained and quite good at what they did. From the perspective of the decision-makers, the ubiquitous 'accounting department' was something of a black box. Nobody really cared what went on in these numbers factories, so long as the numbers that came out of them were accurate.

To a certain extent, accounting remains a laborious, monotonous, and complicated process to this day. Much less so than it once was, however, and the accountants of the world have one man to thank. That man's name is Dan Bricklin.

While watching a lecturer manually write numbers into spreadsheet cells in chalk on a blackboard at Harvard Business School in 1978, Dan Bricklin had an epiphany. As the lecturer changed a figure in one cell on the blackboard, then erased the figures in the subsequent cells, calculating new figures and filling each in again, it occurred to Bricklin (who had experience as a programmer) that this same process could be accomplished using a computer with absolute accuracy and in a fraction of the time.

Inspired, Dan Bricklin spent the next year writing a computer spreadsheet program called VisiCalc, which he unleashed upon the accounting world in 1979. VisiCalc sold over 800,000 copies over the ensuing six years[52].

VisiCalc is widely thought to be computing's first 'killer app' – a software program so essential that you'd buy a computer just to be able to use it[53]. Many did, in fact. Initially, VisiCalc was available only for use on Apple II computers, and more than 25% of the Apple IIs sold in 1979 were reportedly purchased for the express purpose of using VisiCalc. The widespread purchase of a $1,195 computer (about $4125 in 2019 dollars) strictly for the use of a $100 (~$345 in 2019) piece of software stood as a testament to the game-changing power that advancements in technology can bring to common business problems[54].

ANCIENT MARKETERS USED TECH

In the marketing language arena, tech-driven change dates back to the very earliest days of human civilization.

The walls of Pompeii are emblazoned with marketing language advertising a fermented fish stew known as 'garum'. *'Scaurus's best garum, mackerel-based, from Scaurus's manufacturers,'* reads one such slogan – conveniently preserved for eternity by the 79 AD eruption of Mount Vesuvius. Apparently, no one told these ancient marketers that fermented fish stew needs no advertising; it's so delicious it basically sells itself!

Examples of advertising and advertising language can be found spanning the millennia all across the globe, from bronze printing plates for ads for needle shops in China to wall posters on Egyptian papyrus. Advertising, it seems, is as old as commerce itself.

FAST-FORWARD TO THE 15TH CENTURY

It wasn't until the late 15th century, however, when emerging technology began pushing the marketing envelope, and modern advertising language really began to take shape. Gutenberg's invention of the printing press ushered in an era in which it was possible to produce printed material – including commercial advertisements – in large numbers for widespread distribution.

Advertising began to become a much more common practice throughout the world's cities and towns as printing press technology spread. Ads on posters and in newspapers became a ubiquitous presence in most urban centers. As magazines began appearing on the scene in the 17th and 18th centuries, companies quickly began advertising there, too.

The advertisements of this era were almost entirely text-based. The language they used could best be described as 'functional'. Information about various products and services on offer abounded but remained relatively banal and free from the style and sizzle we are familiar with today.

ENTER DIRECT MAIL

Direct mail – advertisements delivered to individual consumers by mail hawking everything from raincoats to medicines – became a common practice in the late 19th century, with brands like Montgomery Ward and Sears making their mark on the scene with the world's first mail-order businesses. It was through these direct mail marketing channels that the art and science of marketing really began to take shape.

Direct mail marketing pioneer Robert Collier's 1937 book *The Robert Collier Letter Book* laid out many of the key marketing principles which foretold how marketing language would evolve in the decades to come.

Here are a few of *The Robert Collier Letter Book*'s most poignant quotes. **In 1937, it was groundbreaking, and forged a new dawn for advertisers around the world – and helped guide me early in my career as a marketer.**

That Robert Collier, he knew a thing or two about copywriting… too bad there was only one of him!

> 'Thousands of sales have been lost, millions of dollars' worth of business have failed to materialize, solely because so few letter writers have that knack of visualizing a proposition – of painting it in words so the reader can see it as they see it.
>
> There are six prime motives of human action: love, gain, duty, pride, self-indulgence, and self-preservation. And frequently they are so mixed together that it is hard to tell which to work on more strongly.
>
> We are credulous people, but we have become so accustomed to hearing everyone claim that his product is the best in the world, or the cheapest, that we take all such statements with a grain of salt.
>
> Rules, however, are merely the start. They are the mechanics of a letter. Real letter-writing only starts there. It is getting the feel of your message that counts.
>
> But do not imagine we were resting on our laurels, or out playing golf all this time. We realized it would not be long until someone caught up to where we were then, so we tried to keep at least one good jump ahead.'

ENTER RADIO AND TV

The advent of the radio in 1895 and the television in 1927 offered intriguing new channels for companies to use to advertise their wares. As these exciting new media claimed pride of place in the world's homes, the golden age of marketing language began.

No longer was it enough to simply offer up an explanation about what your product was and what it could do. Advertising was everywhere. The number of companies flogging this product or that to the masses was growing by the day. **Finding a way to make your product – and your company – stand out from the crowd and capture consumer attention became the order of the day.**

THE BIRTH OF THE ADVERTISING COMPANY

A new entity – the advertising company – arrived on the scene. So began the era of the brand. Brand jingles[55] proliferated on the airwaves, iconic commercials proliferated between (and even during!) your favorite television programs. Billboards began popping up astride highways and byways. Celebrity endorsements, product placement in films and TV, and event sponsorships soon followed.

The language, imagery, and delivery of advertising grew more sophisticated with every passing year.

The best part? It worked.

A well-designed campaign, an unforgettable jingle, a hilarious TV ad, or an effective slogan could quickly propel any brand into the public consciousness. Increased sales and booming revenues followed quickly and predictably.

ENTER THE INTERNET

As the digital age descended upon an unsuspecting public, few anticipated that the World Wide Web was about to change everything. But change everything it did[56]. Personal computers found their way into the homes of millions, opening intriguing new marketing channels, like email, the much-maligned pop-up ad, and the soon ubiquitous banner ad.

Each of these emerging channels demanded its own unique approach to marketing language, and the demand for marketing content, more marketing content, and more marketing content still gave birth to whole new marketing industries.

As the social network pushed its way to the forefront of the human-internet interface, the quest to monetize these platforms through digital marketing began to heat up. The treasure troves of data these platforms had at their disposal opened the door for the targeting and personalization of marketing like never before. The demand for digital marketing content and copy grew exponentially, and armies of

SEO experts, marketing copywriters, and digital marketing specialists rose up to meet it.

With everything progressing so quickly, few brands or marketers had the time or the inclination to step back and take a look at the copy they were using in their marketing and whether or not it was as effective as it could be.

Which brings us to today.

TODAY

The way audiences consume media, marketing, and advertising is in the midst of a seismic shift. Few are left who deny this blatantly obvious modern marketing truth. The digital-first reality in which we are now living has created a demand for marketing and copy that has outstripped our collective ability to meet it.

At the same time, consumer expectations about the quality and relevance of that marketing are shifting quickly. Audiences are demanding more, leaving brands and marketers struggling to catch up. Luckily, emerging technologies are arriving on the scene as we speak, ready to deliver the marketing content required to meet the industry's emerging needs.

Yes, the future of The Language Effect will be tech-driven. Technologies like AI-Powered Copywriting are already paving the way to a more creative future.

“

THE FUTURE OF THE LANGUAGE EFFECT WILL BE TECH-DRIVEN.

”

In this future, customer experience is priority number one. In this future, the relentless churning of more and more marketing copy can be handed over in large part to machines, leaving human creatives to focus on what they're best at – and what machines will never be able to replace – creativity.

Humans and machines will team up to create language models for every brand. A language model that can be applied across every marketing channel to deliver optimal marketing results. For us here at Phrasee, this process often begins with email subject lines, but it certainly doesn't end there.

The day-to-day execution of marketing across multiple channels will be machine-assisted. In many aspects, it already is. The copy that brands use to engage their audiences is simply the next marketing element to embrace this digital marketing fact.

In the ongoing evolution of marketing, some strategies and approaches have stood the test of time. Others have not.

Since the dawn of advertising, we have been seeking ways to do it better. Whether it's garum ads in Pompeii, jingles you can't get out of your head, or a perfectly crafted email in your inbox, your job is to make sure your brand stands out.

Back in the day, your only option was to let humans do all the work. But those days are done – much as accountants were empowered by Excel, marketers of the future are empowered by AI-Powered Copywriting.

And I promise you this: it's far better to be a marketer of the future, than a marketer of the past.

14

MY MARKETING MANIFESTO: ARE YOU A MARKETER OF THE FUTURE?

The preceding pages have been full of ideas – ideas that an elite group of marketers understands. Ideas, many of which are being implemented by the most forward-thinking companies across a range of industries right now. These marketers are not just prescient; they are risk-taking, analytical, and brand-focused. They understand that old ways of thinking just don't cut it anymore. They understand that change is afoot. And they understand they need to lead the change to be able to benefit from it. These are the marketers of the future.

But the big question is: are you going to lead the way… or lag behind your competitors?

I've met thousands of marketers since starting Phrasee in 2015. While each one is undoubtedly beautiful and unique, they generally fall into one of two camps: marketers of the past, or marketers of the future.

Now, of course, nothing is that simple. Such a binary classification isn't reflective of reality, and each of us sits somewhere on the past-future spectrum. Some aspects of each of our marketing practices are historic, and some are futuristic.

But what I've seen is inarguable: the careers of the marketers of the future ascend more quickly than those of the marketers of the past, who tend to stagnate in middle management.

So, what differentiates the marketers of the past from marketers of the future? Well, it's a simple, yet hard distinction. It's obvious, yet opaque. It's quantitative, yet qualitative.

The marketer of the future shines when a situation is ambiguous; when the only way out is to take a risk, they rise to the challenge. They realize that the inertia of the status quo is their biggest obstacle. The marketer of the past, conversely, wants to take last year's plan and tweak it. 'If it ain't broke…' they say, while their innovative competitors reap the rewards.

The marketer of the future doesn't believe in 'failing fast', because all that means is that what they're doing hasn't worked... yet. Their conviction and optimism are their biggest assets, and they don't let isolated incidents cloud the potential of a good idea. On the other hand, the marketer of the past will dip their toes in the ocean, and if the water is a bit cold they'll refuse to go any deeper. They live in fear of making big mistakes, so they never take big chances (and therefore languish in a world of destitute marginality).

The marketer of the future lets their opinions be known to the world. Independent of work duties they'll blog, they'll tweet, they'll speak at conferences, they'll appear on podcasts, and maybe they'll even have their own newsletter. This doesn't mean they're always vocal in meetings – lots of the marketers of the future I've worked with are introverts – but they inherently understand the power of open-sourcing their ideas. However, the marketer of the past is closed to the outside world. They're worried about sharing their knowledge for fear of their competitors using it. They're protective of their tiny kingdom and don't want to let anyone inside the gates. They spend their lives paralyzed by an existential fear of a Trojan horse.

The marketer of the future is incredibly adept at marketing their ideas to their own company and co-workers. They're intuitively persuasive and able to form compelling arguments to get their ideas turned into action. They are not always good at formal business cases – often a bureaucratic crutch of the status quo – but are skilled at persuading people without resorting to politics or paperwork. By contrast, the marketer of the past revels in administrative tasks. They love an RFP and running the process, even though the end result is often just to perpetuate the status quo. Building an accounting-based case is their sweet spot; they don't want to stick their necks out or have to persuade anyone.

When the marketer of the future succeeds, they give credit to their team, or to their vendors, or to their agency. When they fail, they take responsibility and take their lumps. They're intrinsically motivated and understand that all ships will rise with the tide, including theirs. But not the marketer of the past. The marketer of the past will be the first to take credit, but when something goes wrong, they'll either blame another department, one of their vendors, or something else. They're extrinsically motivated, and believe success is a winner-takes-all proposition.

The marketer of the future just looks to their competition or contemporaries for inspiration, although they never ignore what others are doing. They look outside of their industry, even outside of marketing, and get inspired by seemingly unrelated things. They do everything they can to escape echo chambers and are motivated by being the first to do something. On the contrary, the marketer of the past looks at what their competitors or peers do, assumes that these parties must be more advanced than they are, and therefore focuses their efforts on keeping up with the Joneses.

Their biggest motivator is to be slightly less bad than they are now. And that, in my opinion, is a bleak way to live your life.

The marketer of the future understands the incentives of third parties, like agencies and technology vendors, and ensures those incentives are lined up with what they want to achieve. They don't move the goalposts or hold back information; they perceive these third parties as partners, not adversaries, and treat them as such. They make time to meet with agencies and vendors and treat them as equals with equally good ideas to bring to the table. On the flip side is the marketer of the past, who assumes agencies and vendors are always trying to pull a fast one on them and, as a result, keeps them at arm's length. They withhold information, change targets, and don't listen to what they say. The marketer of the past ensures their position of power is paramount in the room, even to the detriment of the end product.

The marketer of the future understands the importance of time. They know that this is their scarcest resource – not money – and realize that delays in getting things done have a huge real – and opportunity – cost. They understand that 20% of the effort gets you 80% of the way there

– and thus incremental effort is of marginal benefit. They don't sacrifice quality – but they realize that perfection is unrealistic. They understand that 'done' is better than 'perfect'. Meanwhile, the marketer of the past won't let anything happen unless there is a 100% chance it's going to go exactly to plan (which, trust me, never happens in the real world). Delays become the norm, or they spend late nights cramming to finish things up when a deadline is fixed. The marketer of the past is usually stressed out, tired, and flustered, though they'll rarely show those qualities externally.

The marketer of the future knows that technology is not a panacea, but they also know it can be very powerful. They hate wasting time doing repetitive tasks, or tasks which humans aren't well suited to perform. And they're not afraid to use technology in ways that may feel uncomfortable to others. They know that technology is coming, and there's nothing they can do about it... so they may as well know how to use it, not fight it. In contrast, the marketer of the past likes things how they are and fights new innovations with skepticism and cynicism. They'll spend their time trying to prove how important they are to the organization as an individual, instead of showing how empowered they and their team are by technology. They would prefer things to stay the same and under their control, instead of accepting that the world – and technology – is always moving forward.

The marketer of the future knows that the digital world runs on language. Whether it's English, or French, or Spanish, or Swahili – the language that people write and speak is what puts dollars in shopping carts. They know that the language they use is the crux of their marketing campaign.

The marketer of the future is ready to embrace the tools at their disposal. They understand that tools like AI, machine learning, and natural language generation aren't here to take anything away from them. They realize that such tools are actually here to give them something: a more efficient, more effective way to do the amazing work that they do.

The marketer of the future understands The Language Effect… and exactly how they can use it to their benefit.

Most importantly of all, 'the marketer of the future' isn't some obscure concept to be realized at some indeterminate future date. The marketers of the future are all around us, plugging away at the marketing problems of the day right this very minute looking for effective ways to solve them. We are they, and they are us.

The marketer of the future is YOU.

15

THAT ALL SOUNDS WONDERFUL

The Language Effect is powerful, and it is everywhere. It's on TV, your phone, and your inbox. In fact, if you've made it this far in this book and you're raring to go – then you're living, breathing proof that The Language Effect works.

And the only durable solution to extend The Language Effect across all your marketing programs is to embrace the future – AI-Powered Copywriting.

Now, of course I'd say that, I'm the AI-Powered Copywriting guy. I came up with the idea, and the phrase. Hell, I've written the book on it.

But this book isn't about me. This book is about my lifelong belief that the language you use in your marketing campaigns deserves more attention. And, that attention simply does not scale if you entrust it to humans.

YOUR COPY WILL MAKE (OR BREAK) YOUR BRAND

The language you use is the crux of marketing. No matter the channel you're using, the copy you select has the power to make you millions – or leave you withering away in obscurity. This isn't (or shouldn't be) news to you.

But, if language is so important, why are there barely any technologies for helping you get better copy? The answer is because it's a hard problem – a very hard problem – to solve. And so instead, many companies and people focus on easier problems. But everyone has mostly solved the easy problems... and it's those who recognize the opportunity The Language Effect represents who will reap the rewards before their competitors.

THE OLD WAYS OF WORKING... AREN'T WORKING

The days of Don Draper dinosaurs dictating your discourse are done. Humans, while awesome at many things, at scale aren't very good at determining what's good copy and what's bad. And even if a few could – there's not enough talent to go around!

Language is complicated, that's for sure. And when you layer your cognitive biases on top of it all, you'll never succeed alone. And, chances are, you're leaving money on the table as a result.

YOUR NEXT STEP IS AI-POWERED COPYWRITING

If you're like most people, you were, at first, flummoxed by the idea of a machine writing better than humans. And you're not alone. But, we trust machines to do all sorts – from a plane's autopilot to recommending TV shows on Netflix. So, it's not too big a stretch to entrust a machine to empower your brand… get you promoted… and make you more money.

'Two words: increased revenue.'

Lee Washington II,
CRM & Loyalty Strategy Manager, JOANN Stores

There are a couple of ways to maximize The Language Effect for your brand. The first way involves shock-and-awing people to respond to you. This is what I call the clickbait race to the bottom. It will get you results in the short term, but will cause real damage to your brand in the long term.

The alternative is to use a long-term strategy enabled by advanced technology, and this is where Phrasee sits. And it's this long-term strategy that is empowering brands around the world, to the tune of millions and millions of dollars in increased revenue.

Of course, here is where I'm supposed to say, 'Now's the time to get in touch with Phrasee[57]!'

BE A MARKETER OF THE FUTURE

AI-Powered Copywriting technology is here, and it's not going away. And it already works awesomely for some of the world's most respected brands.

Some will ignore it and continue down the prehistoric Don Draper route. But these marketers of the past will die out like dinosaurs.

Others, however, will embrace change. They'll understand that the world isn't static – so they can't be either. They'll show courage, and won't be afraid to lead, instead of always following. They'll be the mavens who want to benefit from The Language Effect and will empower their brands with AI-Powered Copywriting. And they'll be leaving their competitors in the dust.

Molly Prosser, during her tenure as creative director at eBay, put it best[58]: 'Technology like Phrasee is to copywriting what Photoshop was to design. And if you're fighting

AI-Powered Copywriting, then you're not thinking creatively enough.'

Molly has captured The Language Effect. And you can too.

ENDNOTES

INTRODUCTION

1. The main thing I did wrong with the statistics was I didn't normalize the data from customer to customer. This meant that some customers were over-represented, and thus skewed the results. So, the statistics the fancy spreadsheet produced were, in the wild, pretty useless. But they sure did pique a lot of curiosity! What's interesting is it was the first research of its kind. Now, everyone does a similar thing, and probably makes the same stupid statistical error I did way back in the day!

2. I actually studied statistics two semesters into my tenure at UVic, but got a D. I re-took it a few years later and got an A+, and as a result can tell you the exact odds of such a miraculous turnaround (spoiler: it's 99% correlated with the associated reduction in partying).

3. True story; you can find the story here, albeit behind a paywall: https://www.ft.com/content/2c3a5bce-e97e-11e2-bf03-00144feabdc0

CHAPTER 1

4. Pagel, Mark. 'Q&A: What is human language, when did it evolve and why should we care?' BMC Biol, 15(64). July 2017. Available at: https://bmcbiol.biomedcentral.com/articles/10.1186/s12915-017-0405-3

5. Fleming, Olivia. 'Reebok forced to pull controversial "Cheat on your girlfriend, not your workout" ad campaign after public backlash'. March 2012. Available at: https://www.dailymail.co.uk/femail/article-2118314/Reebok-forced-pull-controversial-Cheat-On-Your-Girlfriend-Not-Your-Workout-ad-campaign-public-backlash.html

6. Yousuf, Hibah. 'Dumbest moments in business'. CNN Money. December 2011. Available at: https://money.cnn.com/interactive/smallbusiness/dumbest-moments-in-biz/

7. Best Global Brands 2019 Rankings: Apple. 2019. Available at: https://www.interbrand.com/best-brands/best-global-brands/2019/ranking/apple/

8. 'Interbrand Celebrates 20 Years of Best Global Brands Report, Highlights Fastest Growing Sectors.' Interbrand. October 2019. https://www.interbrand.com/newsroom/interbrand-releases-2019-best-global-brands-report/

9. Nicas, Jack. 'Apple is worth $1,000,000,000,000. 20 years ago, it was almost broke'. *The New York Times*. August 2018. Available at: https://www.nytimes.com/2018/08/02/technology/apple-stock-1-trillion-market-cap.html

10. Brooks, Alex. 'Happy 30th Birthday, 1996–2006'. World of Apple. 2006.

11. Holmes, Ryan. 'We now see 5,000 ads a day… and it's getting worse'. LinkedIn Pulse. February 2019. Available at: https://www.linkedin.com/pulse/have-we-reached-peak-ad-social-media-ryan-holmes/ Fun fact: Ryan Holmes, founder of Hootsuite, is, like me, an alum of the University of Victoria.

CHAPTER 3

12. In case you're not sure what a 'secret seed list' is: it's a distribution list for all marketing materials that go to a group of people, without letting the marketers know. It's simply used to give people sh*t when something goes wrong and is, therefore, a massive demotivator. As you may guess, I don't recommend such surreptitious management practices.

13. All of Kait's quotes were taken verbatim from an email exchange in late 2019 – thanks for taking the time, Kait!

14. May the 4th… May the force… get it? So funny. Soooo funny. (Editor's note: it's not funny.)

15. Phrasee has been running this series of parody posts for a few years now, tipping our hats to brands who insist upon using the most niche calendar events as a reason to do marketing, with our tongues firmly implanted in our cheeks.

16. If you don't get the reference, join the club. I'm not a Star Wars guy… but millions seem to be, so if you can't beat 'em…

17. Fun fact: the word 'bollock', a minor English swear word referring to testicles, is legally not considered obscene. The Sex Pistols, upon release of their seminal album, Never Mind the Bollocks, put it to the test in Nottingham Magistrate's Court in 1977.

18. Our included quote is a modern-day version of his Middle English prose. The exact Lydgate quote we leave for historians to argue over – the most pointless, fruitless argument of all time, I presume.

CHAPTER 4

19. Perhaps in the oddest of examples, in the 1980s, Phrasee's chief scientist Dr Neil Yager's father had a pair of 'Where's The Beef' tighty whiteys. Wow.

20. Source: PHOTOCREO Michal Bednarek/Shutterstock.com

21. Smith, Keran. '25 Facebook advertising stats that will blow your mind'. Lyfe Marketing blog. August 2019. Available at: https://www.lyfemarketing.com/blog/facebook-advertising-statistics/

CHAPTER 5

22. Nieva, Richard. 'Facebook says Cambridge Analytica had data on 87 million people'. Cnet. April 2018. Available at: https://www.cnet.com/news/facebook-says-cambridge-analytica-had-data-on-87m-people/

23. Yes, I know, I'm bored of hearing about GDPR as well. I promise that this is the only reference in this entire book to the GDPR. But we have to mention it at least once, I'm pretty sure that's the law, right?

CHAPTER 6

24. Levy, Erin. *Mad Men*. Season 6, Episode 4. April 2013

25. Some may argue that focus groups were the scientific mechanism of the day. But time and time again, focus groups have been proven to be unreliable and prone to bias, groupthink, and ethical complications. There are studies that insist focus groups are effective; many of these studies are, by sheer coincidence I'm sure, funded by focus group providers. Hmmm…

26. It's a scientific fact that you shouldn't trust anyone under 30, and you should never trust anyone over 30.

27. Myers, Dan. 'How Much a Dozen Eggs Cost the Year You Were Born'. The Daily Meal. August 2019. Available at: https://www.thedailymeal.com/eat/egg-price-year-you-were-born-gallery

28. Uren, Amanda. 'Photoshop before Photoshop'. Mashable. Feb 2015. Available at: https://mashable.com/2015/02/19/before-photoshop/?europe=true

29. The Radicati Group. Email statistics report. 2016.

30. Facebook Quarterly report. February 2019.

CHAPTER 7

31. It will never cease to annoy me that 'phonetics' is not spelled phonetically. Stupid humans.

32. Tougaw, Jason. 'The reading brain'. *Psychology Today*. Oct 2018. Available at: https://www.psychologytoday.com/gb/blog/the-elusive-brain/201810/the-reading-brain

33. A portmanteau is itself, a portmanteau. Isn't that linguistically delicious, or as I like to say, linguicious!

34. Yes, I know that an apostrophe is not the correct punctuation here, because 'charlatans' is a plural noun and isn't in a possessive form. But I hope that the grammar nerds reading that sentence will become

incensed by my cavalier use of that apostrophe, until they read this endnote, and realize they've been had!

35. Fun fact: when using bad grammar on Twitter, there is a 98.6% chance that someone will point out your error.

36. Yes, this is incorrect grammar. But, as Eric B and Rakim made famous in the 80s, you understand the gist, despite its colloquialisms and double negatives – and that's the power of language.

37. This is something that high technology is much more suited to than humans… for example – AI-Powered Copywriting – but more on that later.

CHAPTER 8

38. Keillor, Garrison. 'In Search of Lake Wobegon'. *National Geographic Magazine.* December 2000.

39. McCormick IA, Walkey FH, Green DE. 'Comparative perceptions of driver ability: a confirmation and expansion'. June 1986. In Gose, Tia. 'Why we're all above average'. *Live Science.* February 2013.

40. Shedler, Jonathan; Martin Mayman; Melvin Manis. 'The "Illusion" of Mental Health'. *American Psychologist.* 1993.

41. As it turns out, I almost did get fired for that typo – but never learned that until years later. Sometimes, you're just better off not knowing the truth, sheltered (and perhaps biased) from the harsh realities of life.

CHAPTER 9

42. All prices were taken from https://uk.finance.yahoo.com/

43. Hammett, Ellen. 'Adidas reduces focus on short-term metrics as it looks to protect brand health'. *Marketing Week*. May 2019. Available at: https://www.marketingweek.com/adidas-reduces-focus-short-term-marketing/

44. Graham, Megan. 'Old Navy will shift back to brand-building in a growing trend among advertisers'. CNBC. Nov 2019. Available at: https://www.cnbc.com/2019/11/22/old-navy-was-neglecting-brand-marketing-gap-cfo-admits.html

CHAPTER 11

45. A better description of his patented invention, the SlipStream, can be found here, although if you're like me you'll probably understand, at most, about 2% of it: https://www.globalmethane.org/documents/events_oilgas_20070115_15jan07-remvue_energy_optimization_and_slipstream.pdf

46. To read an interview with my dad, if you're interested, go here: https://www.sfu.ca/science/alumni-community/inspiring-alumni1/profiles/howard-malm.html

47. You can find out more about my dad's scholarship here: https://www.sfu.ca/dean-gradstudies/awards/privateawards/all-awards/HowardMalm.html

CHAPTER 12

48. Fun fact: the odds of hitting black thirteen are 37-1. But casinos generally only payout 35-1. The lesson? Don't play roulette.

49. Fun fact: Phrasee was the first UK tech company to close a venture capital funding round after the Brexit referendum in 2016. Not bad for me, Phrasee's leader, one of those damned job-stealing immigrants!

50. When we first started, we thought there would be some open-source libraries we could use to expedite our development. But nope! There was simply nothing out there that was anywhere near good enough for our needs. So instead we built our NLG system 100% by ourselves, one line of code at a time.

CHAPTER 13

51. I'm joking! Of course, the moon landing wasn't faked... right?

52. Licklider, Tracy Robert. 'Ten Years of rows and columns'. *Byte*. 13 pp. 324 – 331. 1989.

53. Harford, Tim. 'How computing's first "killer app" changed everything'. BBC News. May 2019. Available at: https://www.bbc.co.uk/news/business-47802280

54. Brandel, Mary. 'PC Software Transforms The PC'. *PC Magazine*. Aug 1999. p. 62.

55. If you want proof of how well a solid jingle works: find your office's token Canadian (every office has one, it seems). Say to them the words: 'Sleep Country Canada.' And if they don't break into song and sing, 'Why buy a mattress anywhere else?' then the chances are they're identity thieves and not Canadian at all.

56. I'd be remiss to not include a link to Avenue Q's seminal internet ballad 'The Internet is for Porn'. It's true in some ways – much of the innovation in digital marketing stems from the porn and gambling industries since they need to operate outside the boundaries of common practice to succeed. So, what I'm saying, obviously, is you should gamble more and watch porn more. Anyways, here's that song: https://www.youtube.com/watch?v=LTJvdGcb7Fs&t=5s

CHAPTER 15

57. Sales 101 amirite? But seriously, go to: phrasee.co/book-a-demo

58. You can listen to the full interview with Molly Prosser at: thelanguageeffect.com

Printed by Amazon Italia Logistica S.r.l.
Torrazza Piemonte (TO), Italy

12687022R00112